PAROLE YOURSELF

*Free yourself from fear and self-doubt
to live the life of success and abundance you deserve*
Wade Hoover

To Mom and Dad,

Without your unwavering love and support, I don't know where I would be. I certainly would not be a writer. You have always been there for me and I realize that your efforts have been Herculean in their scope. I know I have always been quite a challenge. I love you with all my heart, and I am grateful for all of your patience over the years. It would not be possible to repay you for all you have done and all you mean to me. You are quite simply, the best!

Thank you! I love you!

Parole Yourself Copyright © 2018

by Wade Hoover. All Rights Reserved.

All rights reserved. No part of this book may be reproduced in any form or by any electronic or mechanical means including information storage and retrieval systems, without permission in writing from the author. The only exception is by a reviewer, who may quote short excerpts in a review.

Wade Hoover
Printed in the United States of America

First Printing: 2018

ISBN: 9781981064991

CONTENTS

Introduction
Chapter 1: The Question is: Why?
Chapter 2: Luck is a Lie
Chapter 3: Successful People Fail More
Chapter 4: The World is NOT Falling Apart
Chapter 5: The Comfort Zone
Chapter 6: Success is a Choice
Chapter 7: Self-Talk
Chapter 8: The Law of Attraction
Chapter 9: Faith
Chapter 10: Conquering Fear and Worry
Chapter 11: Everyone Pays Their Dues
Chapter 12: Create a Habit of Success
Chapter 13: To Have More You Must BE More
Chapter 14: Naysayers
Chapter 15: Your Three Gifts Make You Unstoppable
Chapter 16: Self-Discipline – The Next 30 Minutes
Chapter 17: Don't be a Squirrel
Chapter 18: Fit for Success
Chapter 19: The Right Time to Quit
Chapter 20: Parole Yourself

Introduction

You *can* live life on your terms. You *can* be happy and fulfilled. You *can* wake up excited for the day. You *can* have all of these things. However, if you are not currently living the life you want to live, don't worry. Things are about to change.

Sadly, most people feel like their lives are not working out the way they had hoped. They feel as though they are missing out - that a joyful life is for others. They feel that success is out of their reach. You may feel like this too. I understand. I understand because that is how I felt for so many years.

I felt like I was jinxed. It seemed that nothing I ever did was right. I felt like, no matter how hard I tried, nothing ever worked out, and that I was destined to live a life of struggle. But - I was wrong!

I have learned that we all have much more control over our lives than we typically realize. Now that I know what we are all capable of, I want to share it with everyone.

You have struggled (without your deserved reward) long enough. You can make a significant change in your life, and you can make that change today! I will show you how. This is no joke! This is not some esoteric, mystical idea. I have found a simple and logical path to success.

The most successful people in the world have understood the information in this book. Successful people have learned these simple ideas as they worked for what they wanted. I have learned in the same way, by making mistakes and trying again.

This information has been presented here to help you live the life you want to live. I have been through the struggles. I have learned how to make them pay off. Now you too can reap the benefits of your struggles, rather than being dissuaded by them. You may have some more struggle ahead, but this time, those struggles will lift you up – not knock you down.

I'm sure you have heard people say, *"I went to the school of hard knocks."* I realized something over the years. EVERYONE goes to the school of hard knocks (S.O.H.K.). The problem is, not everyone graduates. Life is a tremendous teacher. We merely need to learn.

When I say that not everyone graduates from the S.O.H.K. I mean that, although everyone struggles in life, not everyone learns from these struggles. If we do not learn from our struggles, and apply what we have learned, we will not graduate, from the struggle, to the rewarding life we want. We will remain within the struggle.

It took me a long time to obtain my degree from the S.O.H.K. However, I finally applied what I have learned. I have now experienced success - professionally, financially, creatively, physically, and emotionally.

I now know what it takes to succeed. It is not as complicated as so many people think. Once you understand a few simple concepts, and apply a few, new, easy-to-use, tools to your daily life, you will see that you can live the life you have always wanted to live.

You will be able to free yourself from the stress and worry that has held you back for far too long. You can do this! You deserve this! You have the ability - right now, to change everything. Do it! Parole Yourself, and free yourself from fear and self-doubt to live the life of success and abundance you deserve.

1.
The Question is - Why?

That is one powerful question. Why? Why did I write this book? Why are you reading this book?

I can tell you why I wrote this book. The answer is quite simple, I care. That's about as simple and accurate as you can get. I care. I care about people. I care about you. I want you to be happy and fulfilled. Why? Because I know what it's like to be unhappy.

I know what it's like to struggle. I know what it's like to live in a constant state of worry. I know what it's like to feel like a failure. I know what it's like to feel as though I am worthless. I know what it's like to feel like I'm letting everyone down. I know what it feels like to be stuck and believe that there is no way out. And - I know what it's like to escape!

Have you have ever felt any of these feelings? If you have ever felt this way, or if you feel this way now - hang on! Everything is about to change! You will see that you are capable of freeing yourself from these feelings and the limitations they can cause. You are ready to parole yourself and live!

I am 53 years old, and I spent most of my life believing that I was somehow jinxed. I thought I was not good enough to live the life I wanted to live, and I even began to feel like luck was always against me. Nothing could be further from the truth. I just couldn't see it. It's strange how life works. For me, the worst day of my life led me to be the very best version of myself.

On August 2nd, 2016, my life changed forever. My world had been turned upside-down, and it was time for me to announce *"last call"* for my pity-party. My eyes had been opened. I lost my 23-year-old nephew to addiction. I thought that loss would break me. Losing someone you are close to, especially someone so young, is devastating.

I was crushed, and I couldn't get my mind around how this could have happened. I was angry and hurt. Like most people in that situation, I kept trying to figure out what I could have done differently. Could I have done something? Could I have said something that would have prevented this from happening?

After two weeks of torturing myself with these thoughts, I realized that it doesn't make any difference now. The simple fact was, it was just too late. He was gone, forever. Forever. It's still difficult. I had to walk away while writing this. I suppose the pain will remain forever.

What now? I realized that there was nothing I could do for my nephew. It was too late. But what I could do, was spend the rest of my life helping as many people as possible. I will help in the way I know best. I will share what life has spent over 50 years beating into my thick skull!

Life is always teaching us. I did not realize that simple fact for many years. Once I decided I wanted to help others, I began to reflect on my life. I looked at my successes, my failures, and all the struggles. I began to understand the lessons, that I didn't even know I was learning. I began to read books written by successful people, and I began listening to them speak. Yes! I thought. Yes! I get it!

I was beginning to read and hear accomplished people saying the very things that I had begun thinking. I started to realize that all of us, no matter how different we may seem, share many common thoughts, worries, hopes, and dreams. We are more alike than we realize.

At work, my attitude became more positive. And I was finding more ways to contribute. My boss typically had me speak to the department when we had full department meetings. She said, *"You're our best speaker."* That was cool. On a few occasions, I was asked to get the team pumped up. That was fun, and it seemed effective. I was even asked to speak to the sales team when they were going through a bit of a drought. That went extremely well, and I thought, maybe I'm on to something here.

I thought it might be a good idea to become a motivational speaker. Why not? I wanted to help people. I have a great deal of experience in taking on challenges, and I really cannot shut up . . . ever. So, I got started.

I began volunteering. I started speaking to young people. I spoke to inner-city teens in Philadelphia who wanted to go to college. I Spoke to at-risk youths in detention centers and at schools to help these young people build the confidence they need to go after their dreams.

I have found my dream. I didn't know there could be something that would bring me such joy. Watching people's faces light up when I share something that resonates with them is more rewarding than I could have imagined. When I see that light go on, and I know that they get it, I feel an instant high. They look so happy. I love that moment.

There's nothing like standing up in front of a crowd, that you can see is somewhat less than excited, (#salesteam) and then watch them as they get pumped up. To see them laughing, excitedly, and high-fiving each other after you speak is a blast. Yeah, I'm a rock star. Just sayin' (Anyone buying that?)

Listen, you need to have fun in life. I am very serious about the content of this book, but I have to be me. I hope that works for you. As you read through this book, I hope you feel inspired. I hope you draw strength and confidence as you move from chapter to chapter.

Deep down, I truly believe that you can be as successful as you wish to be. The idea that your success is in your hands has been proven many times over. I hope you get something meaningful from the pages that follow. I hope you have some fun reading this as well.

This brings me to the second "Why?" Why are you reading this book? What do you hope to get out of this? I simply want you to keep that thought in the back of your mind. What is interesting to me, is how various people take different things away from my speeches. We tend to process things in our own way. We also tend to use what we have learned in very different ways.

I say learned, but not because I am here to be a teacher. No. I am here to act as the catalyst that motivates you to learn about yourself. The greatest lesson life has taught me is that we constantly underestimate ourselves. I will do everything in my power to help you break free and see your true potential. Each of us has so much more within us than we realize. If you don't see it now, you will by the time you finish reading this book. I have faith in you, and soon, you will too.

2.
Luck is a Lie

To be free to achieve your goals, you need to free yourself of the lies that hold others back. These lies are excuses, and excuses do not yield results.

It takes a lot to be successful in life. Whether it be in the corporate world, entrepreneurship, education, entertainment, whatever path you choose, you'll need a number of things if you want to succeed. But there is one thing I hear mentioned all the time. The one thing that people seem to think of as most important is, actually, the last thing you need to worry about. That thing is - luck.

The idea that luck is the secret to success is a lie. I cannot tell you how frustrated I get when I hear people say that successful people are lucky. This is unfair, it's an excuse, and it is flat-out wrong! Let's take a closer look at the idea that success is a matter of luck. I think you'll get a better picture that way.

When you say that someone is successful because they *"got lucky,"* this dismisses all the work, all the risk, and all the sacrifices that were made on the way to their success. Make no mistake. These elements were substantial.

Let's start with an easy one. Anyone can understand that a student who earns a PhD. did not get lucky. There is no way that a fortunate event was responsible for a student fulfilling all the responsibilities associated with higher education. Everyone realizes that the work had to be done.

We have all attended school, and we have all experienced varying levels of success. We have first-hand knowledge of academic challenges. The fact that success in school requires effort over time is easily understood and accepted by just about everyone. This doesn't seem to be the case in other challenging areas of life. Why?

In the corporate world, people see that others have succeeded where they, themselves, have not. For some reason, many employees feel that there is something unfair going on at work. Some of you reading this could be thinking, *"You're darned right there is something going on at my office!"* Well, maybe that's true, and maybe it's not. Let's dig a little deeper.

When someone climbs the ladder, from entry-level to upper management in an organization, it takes a serious commitment. This kind of success requires great effort and consistency over an extended period. It takes a proper attitude, intelligence, social skills, and great sacrifice. While nearly everyone would like this type of success, most are not willing to do what is required to earn that success.

Unfortunately, there are a lot of employees out there who insist that the road to success is back-stabbing, cutting corners, lying and kissing . . . well, you know. Some are willing to do this. They may have short-term success but, typically, these folks are found-out to be exactly who they are. At that point, it will go badly for them.

I am sure you have known people like this. You may have even seen them being escorted out of the office, red-faced, carrying a box of personal items to their car. That is typically how this scenario ends.

Some of you may believe that the way described above is the way to get ahead, but declare, *"I won't do that!"* That's a good thing. However, if you refuse to behave, in that way, but insist that this is the only way to get ahead, you need to look inward. Why do you hold this attitude? Do you say these things because you believe them to be true? Or, are you simply alleviating yourself of all responsibility to make a true commitment?

Often, taking the stance that cheating is the only way to succeed, declaring *"I won't do that,"* is merely a way that people try to claim a moral high-ground. This is usually done for one of two reasons. It is either to cover for their fear of failure or because they are simply too lazy to put in the effort. They use this as a reason to not even try to succeed – to quit before they start.

I want you to be on the lookout for these behaviors in yourself. You will never get ahead if you make excuses. Excuses don't get results - effort does. Getting ahead the *right way* will be more rewarding. It takes commitment and a good attitude to succeed. These things are completely within your control. Let me share a story with you.

I had been hired as a copywriter. My job was to write websites for small businesses. This was a temporary position, and it was to last three to six months. There was the possibility that some writers, who performed well enough, would be hired full-time at the end of the six months. This position was on the second-shift team. We were to work from 3:30 PM to 12:00 midnight, Monday through Friday.

This was a relatively small team, with less than 20 employees at the start. Most of these employees were permanent, full-time employees, and most of them had been with the company for at least two-to-four years. There were only a handful of us (new) temps. I knew only two things for sure: I needed to be hired full-time, (I had become accustomed to living indoors, and I wanted that to continue.) and I didn't know what I was doing . . . at all.

I was the oldest person on the team. I had grown up without any technology other than a black and white television and a rotary phone. (Young folks may have to Google that one.) Computers were very new to me. The rest of the team grew up with them and were quite proficient. Was I in over my head? It sure seemed that way.

From the very beginning, I was asking questions. I was always bugging someone about how to do this or that. So . . . um, how do I access my email? (Wow) I was truly a fish out of water. It didn't help that the company's systems were out of date and didn't communicate with each other. Even people with solid computer skills had difficulty learning all the systems and how they needed to be accessed and used.

Writing a website was daunting. The writing part wasn't so bad, but all the other stuff was brutal. We had to go into one system after another just to grab the account and the information we needed in order to do the work. Then, we had to repeatedly update multiple trackers. After that, we needed to go into the platform where we would be writing the site. (This platform liked to shut down on us each day.) Once in the platform, we were to create the template, add all the client information, build the pages, and then we were ready to write the site. This was exhausting.

I used to explain writing a website like this. *"It's as if you want to make a ham sandwich, and step one is, build a deli."* (You get the idea.) Also, each employee was required to write two websites per day. Once the website had been written, we had to call the client and see if they liked their new site. If not, we would have to make as many changes as they wanted before the site went "live" online.

One more thing - I couldn't type. I still can't. I am actually hunt-and-pecking my way through this book. OK. Now, the stage is set.

Every day at work, I was asking full-time employees questions. Now that you understand what our responsibilities were, you can guess how happy they were to stop what they were doing to help out the old guy who is learning computers as he goes. I could sense that I was a bit of an intrusion. I did hate bothering them, but I couldn't afford to fail. I needed this job.

Over the next few months, I began to improve, and I asked fewer questions. I was getting the hang of my job, and I was doing well. The company decided to expand and bring in more temps to the second shift. The team was growing rather quickly. This was a good sign, I thought. Maybe this improves my chance of being made a permanent, full-time employee. Or maybe, they are trying to find stronger candidates to join the company full-time. I didn't know. But I kept working.

The new people were having many issues, just like I did when I started. I know that the full-timers didn't have time to work with them all. I felt bad for these new people. I remembered what it was like, when I was just starting out, and I wanted to help. I spent a lot of time each night going from one desk to another and another to offer assistance. When I returned to my desk, I often found two or three people waiting for me. Oh boy. How am I going to get MY work done?

To keep up with my productivity, I had to work through breaks. We were required to take a half-hour lunch, so I clocked out for a half-hour, but I continued working through lunch. I would also clock out at the end of my shift and continue working until I had completed my responsibilities for the day.

During this time, my boss, a young woman (half my age), sat behind me. Her name was Jenn. We didn't talk that much at first. She had just been promoted, and she was very busy with a growing team of newbies. We would later become good friends.

The team was growing fast, and we were going to need some new managers at some point. One day, Jenn sent out an email to the team. She wanted to mentor someone. She wanted to show someone on the team the ropes of management. This was how she learned. She asked that anyone interested send her an email, and let her know why they would make a good manager. I sent her an email. (Was I getting ahead of myself?)

A few weeks later, we had a team meeting. Jenn told us she had made her decision on who she would mentor. She said my name. The team applauded. Huh? ME? What just happened? She looked at me with a big smile. I guess she could see the surprise on my face. She turned to the team and said, *"How many of you have been saved by Wade?"* I watched as all the hands went up. Jenn looked at me and smiled again. I couldn't believe it.

After the meeting, Jenn pulled me aside. She said, *"You do all of your work, you're great with the clients on the phone, and every time I look up, you're helping somebody. It's like you have your own team already. Everyone comes to you. To me, that just screams management."*

Within the next six months, I was made full-time and promoted to Associate Manager. I interviewed and hired a team of 30 new employees. They were amazing! I loved that team and they NEVER, EVER let me down.

So, what is my point? What does all of this have to do with luck? Exactly. It has nothing to do with luck. That's the point. At that time, some people, those who were with the company for years, may have thought that my promotion was unfair. After all, they were there longer. I had just learned how to do the job that they were doing so well before I was hired, and I had to learn from **them**. How did I get promoted before they did?

Many people in their spot may think that Jenn played favorites, or that I did something to undermine them. The reality is simple. I tried my best to help the new people to learn and to feel comfortable. I refused to let them feel like a burden. This took considerable effort. It was not easy to keep up with my work, but I knew what they were going through, and I knew I could help.

That's what I want you to see. I used this example not to pat myself on the back, (OK. Just a little.) but to illustrate a point. The truth is, when someone seems to get more than someone else, it doesn't necessarily mean that they did something underhanded or that they were lucky. I always have, and I always will, believe that hard work and doing what you know to be right, is the best way to get ahead.

What I experienced, reinforced my belief that, *if you do what you know to be right, things will go well for you.* I was surprised that Jenn had chosen me. There were plenty of candidates that were more experienced, smarter, and faster. What she saw though, was that I cared.

Over the years, she mentioned that to me repeatedly. She told me that my team performed so well because they could see that I cared about them. One woman on my team told me. *"You are the very definition of leading by example."* I get choked up just thinking about this wonderful team. Is it any wonder that I loved them?

During some high-pressure times, my team was asked to perform at a level that, even upper management admitted, was unreasonable. They set production numbers that they knew couldn't, realistically, be reached. But they said we needed to do our best to attempt to reach these goals. I asked my team to try to hit those numbers. They exceeded their goal - by far!

Upper management would continually praise me for my team's success. I ALWAYS corrected them. I told them the truth. I just had great people. They deserved the praise. They did the work. They were NOT *lucky*. Their success was a matter of consistent, hard work. Consistent, hard work . . . hmm, could that be important?

A quick note: Hard work pays off. Jenn started out in that company at the lowest possible level. She was promoted at least five times and had her own department. She was managing nearly 200 people, and at least 6 managers, before a former executive hired her away. After less than one year at her new company, she has been given several new teams to run over several cities, country-wide. Wow. She must be really lucky!

When people in the public eye make it really big, most people don't truly appreciate what it took for them to get there. They didn't see the long road of effort, rejection, and sacrifice.

The world of entertainment has great examples of people who seemed to just get out of bed one day, get on a stage and become a mega-star. The reality is not even close. Comedienne Wanda Sykes is a great example of what it takes to become an overnight success.

I remember the first time I saw comedienne Wanda Sykes. Years ago, I saw Wanda on television. She was appearing on her first cable special. I had no idea who this woman was, but I gave her a shot. I watched her one-hour special. She was awesome! I laughed my butt off!

This was the first time I saw Wanda, but it would certainly not be the last. She suddenly showed up everywhere. She was on T.V., in movies, and even hosted the Oscars! It all seemed to happen *"overnight."* How could someone, who no one had ever heard of, just show up one day and be everywhere? If you're good, I guess it happens right away for you - right? Ha-ha, not even close!

In an interview, Wanda was asked what it was like to be an overnight success. Wanda intimated that her overnight success actually took her about twenty years.

Stand-up comedy is one of the toughest games around. The journey is long and tedious. The competition is cut-throat. In order to make it in comedy, you have to start out at open mic night. I have done this. It is brutal. You show up at a local comedy club and sign up to perform. When you are starting out, no one knows you. You will go on last. That means you may sit and watch 25 *"comedians"* perform before you get to go on stage. You suffer through hours of really bad attempts at comedy. By the time you go on stage, all the comedians who went before you, and their friends, have already gone home. You get to perform before, (I've done this) 8 people who just want to go home.

After about two hours of torture, you get 4 minutes on stage in front of 8 people. By the time you get home, you'll get about four hours of sleep before you have to get up for work. You will probably be doing this several times a week for the first year or two. That's the best-case scenario. Then, one day, you get a break! You get paid to do 10 minutes on a Saturday night!

"Awesome!" You think, *"$80.00! When do they shoot my E! True Hollywood story? Oh. Not just yet?"* No. Not yet. Now you get to spend 10-20 years developing your craft and trying to make a name for yourself. You drive hundreds of miles to get on stage at small clubs in front of small crowds for small pay. Sometimes, the pay doesn't cover what you spent on gas to get there.

This is a life of sacrifice, hard work, and rejection. Most comedians quit after a few years. Some try longer, but eventually move on to something else. But some . . . some are willing to fight.

Some refuse to give up no matter how hard it gets. Some, like Wanda, have made a commitment to their dream and absolutely refuse to quit. They work and work and keep moving forward no matter how many times they get knocked down. Their desire is stronger than their fears. It is stronger than their obstacles. Their drive pushes them through all adversity. They truly want it, and so they will not stop until they make their dream a reality.

Then, one day, after all the struggle, sacrifice, pain, disappointment and tears - the ones who really want it, make it. And when they finally make it to the top, when all the struggles finally pay off, there will always be those who say, *"Wow, must be nice to be so lucky."* Amazing.

There will always be a moment that you can point to in any successful career where you can say, *"Ha! See that. There is the lucky break that set this person's career on track for amazing success. Without this, they would not have made it!"* Sadly, people use this as an argument for the idea that success is a matter of luck. It is a flawed argument.

The truth is, we make our own luck. In later chapters, I will share with you a story where I made my own luck. (It's pretty cool, so you'll want to read on.) But I digress. When I say we make our own luck, I mean that, when we make a true commitment to a goal and work tirelessly toward that end, we create more opportunities. There will be many moments of bad luck, first. But, if we keep going when others quit, we will be the ones who finally get that break.

Those who didn't have the courage to continue, will point to that one moment, that one break, and say that we were lucky. They will say that they could have made it too, if only they had gotten that break. Well, maybe they would have - if they hadn't quit. Or maybe they didn't quit, but perhaps they didn't work hard enough, or take enough chances.

Fortune favors the **bold**, not the hopeful. The secret to success is hard work and determination. These two elements will eventually lead to the lucky break you are looking for. Any other interpretation of luck is a lie. Keep reading, you'll see what I mean.

3.
Successful People Fail More

Something that often surprises people when I say it is, *"successful people fail far more often than unsuccessful people."* On the surface that sounds crazy, doesn't it? But it makes perfect sense when you look at their behaviors. There is one very simple reason that successful people fail more, and it is something that we can all profit from understanding.

The reason successful people fail more often than unsuccessful people is - successful people take more risks. The more risks you take, the more opportunity you have to fail. That's just logical. What is most important, however, is that you will have more opportunities to succeed.

There is an interesting dynamic at work here. It is easy to predict who will succeed and who will not. It has nothing to do with one's station in life. That has been proven time and again. Even those who have come from the humblest of beginnings have accomplished some of the most amazing things in sports, art, business, education, innovation, etc. Too many people have gone from poverty to becoming millionaires for anyone to logically believe that someone's current situation will stop them from succeeding.

It is also not a matter of luck, as mentioned before. Luck is the byproduct of consistent, hard work. It would be unfair to attribute the success of someone who has spent years toiling, struggling, and continuing toward their goal, undaunted by repeated failures, to mere luck. When they get a fortunate break, this is not an instance of luck, but rather the result of grinding one's way through all the misfortune to finally strike opportunity. This is the *creation* of opportunity, not the stumbling upon good fortune.

Once that break comes along, it is typically only the dedicated who will fully capitalize on that opportunity. Those who work the hardest to create opportunity will be the least likely to waste it. They have put so much effort in already that they want to make the most of any chance they get to move closer to their goal.

If it is not one's starting point or simple good fortune that produces success, what then is the obvious catalyst that makes predicting who will succeed, so easy. What element do the successful possess that propel them to the top while others struggle? Is there one element? Is it really so easy to predict who will succeed and who will not? The answer, for me, is yes.

There is, in my opinion, one, simple trait that all successful people possess. With this very simple but spectacularly powerful trait, anyone can create tremendous success for themselves. The best part? Anyone can possess this trait. Sadly, too few do.

So, what is this magical element? (The suspense is killing you. I know.) OK. The major difference between the successful and the unsuccessful is merely - *attitude*. I know you were hoping for some earth-shattering, mystical, magical answer for the ages, but I am here to share the truth. I want to share what I have spent over 50 years learning. I am sharing this because I want you to live the life you want to live, the life you *deserve* to live! Please be patient, and open your mind to this simple idea.

Attitude is everything. When I say attitude I mean, the *proper* attitude. You need to have a positive, can-do attitude, of course. But there is more. You must have the attitude that says, *"I will do this thing, and I will not stop, no matter what, until I achieve my goal."*

You need the attitude that will carry you through the tough times. You need to maintain belief and commitment no matter how bleak things seem. Many people, sadly, quit on themselves, never knowing if that big break was just one day away. Let me show you how this repeatedly plays out.

Most people set out, at one time or another, to try to accomplish something in life. This could be anything. The goal really doesn't matter. The process is our focus here. Let's say, for the sake of this example, that two people, Jack and Alan, (I used these names because I do not know a Jack or an Alan. They are not males for any reason in particular. These principles seem to apply to everyone equally.) each decided to start a small landscaping business.

Jack and Alan live in the same town, but they do not know each other, and they know nothing of each other's business plans. These two individuals seem very similar, but they are very different in one specific way. While they are both white males in their mid-20s, and come from similar blue-collar backgrounds, they have very different aspirations and attitudes.

They each want to own their own landscaping business, but they have different visions for the business, and they each have very different motives. Alan sees an opportunity in his hometown to create a thriving business that will be adaptable to the needs of the growing community. Jack doesn't like being told what to do and wants to make his own hours.

You can see that each of these two individuals wants to be their own boss, but for very different reasons. Alan wants to control his own destiny and provide a quality service to the community. He sees the opportunity for growth. Jack wants to avoid having responsibility thrust upon him by a boss.

Alan is thinking forward. He craves the challenge and wants to build something meaningful. Jack wants to avoid being challenged. Having his own business is an escape. I have seen these two approaches in real life. The results are quite predictable.

As you read this, I suspect you are thinking of people in your life. I suspect you know an Alan or a Jack. Maybe this reminds you of yourself. These two fictional characters are composites of real people. I know how this works out for these two. I am sure you can guess as well.

When deciding to take on a challenge, it is extremely important that you have the proper attitude going in. You need to be strong-willed, confident, and willing to face disappointment and setbacks. If you take on a significant challenge without a true commitment to success, you will not succeed. You will be challenged. You will need to make sacrifices. You will suffer.

If you are like Jack and take on a significant challenge without bringing significant *will*, the results are not difficult to guess. If you look at a challenge realistically, as an opportunity to achieve, your chance of success will increase. If you decide that you are willing to commit to your dream, fully, you WILL succeed. It may not happen right away. There will be tough times ahead, but if you accept that and are willing to fight through the tough times, you will absolutely be rewarded for your efforts.

Alan shares the mindset of the successful, and jack does not. Alan is destined to succeed. He will succeed, not because he is lucky or because he has any built-in advantages, but because he has a vision. He has a dream. Jack does not. Jack, simply wants to be able to make some money and hopefully sleep-in on rainy days. I have actually seen these two approaches in action.

The "Jack" character in our story will sleep-in often. He will do the work that is available. He will do what is necessary to pay his bills and have some spending money. Jack will spend his money as soon as he gets it. I have seen this many times. Jack will always have cash on hand. When it rains, you will see his truck parked in front of a bar. (#Truestory).

Alan rises early, seven days a week. He is never late to a job-site or to meet with a client. His clothes are clean, and he is always clean-shaven (Does Jack own a razor?) and well-mannered. When Alan gets money, it goes directly into the business account. Alan always has his mind on marketing and business upgrades. Before long, Alan will have an office and a garage for equipment. Jack has a drawer in his bedroom filled with *"tax stuff."* All of Jack's equipment still sits in the back of his pickup truck, with a tarp covering it, to keep the rain off.

Six years later, Alan has 11 trucks and 25 employees. Jack now works for Alan. But for how long? He was late again.

As I said, this story is a composite of several actual stories. The names, and some details, have been changed to preserve anonymity. I needed to share this story. I wanted to help you visualize the journey a little bit. Now I want to elaborate on the process for the successful and unsuccessful and how they end up where they always seem to end up.

I will show you how attitude dictates behavior and how this behavior determines success. Think of the people in your life. Think of their attitudes and behaviors and think about your own. I am certain that you will be able to identify these behaviors in those around you and in yourself. You will begin to understand how it is easy to predict who will succeed and who will fail. A consistent attitude and behavior will tell the tale.

When people set out to achieve a goal, they have an idea about what they want to make happen. They take their first steps forward. They try something new. The successful and unsuccessful alike will try . . . once. What happens next will make all the difference. When people set out to do something. There will be challenges. There will always be some failures. Here is where we separate the Alans from the Jacks.

At the first failure, Jack gets upset. He makes an excuse for his failure. He will not take responsibility. He will blame anything, or anyone, he can for his failure. The failure will be the responsibility of someone who didn't treat him right, the bank, his clients, the economy, his lack of good fortune or resources. He will look everywhere but in the mirror. You see, it's just not Jack's fault. How could it be? He did everything right. Right?

You see, Jack did not make the commitment. He didn't *really* want success. He would have liked it, but he did not *really want it*. He will try to convince anyone who will listen, how hard he worked and how he sacrificed so much. But you know the truth. He *sort'a* had a business. He *kind'a* made an effort. But the reality is, he wasn't willing to go through the pain and suffering necessary to achieve great things. Alan was different.

Alan had some trouble too. He planned ahead and did all the research and all the legwork. He had some good commercial contracts lined up to start the season. However, two very important, contracts fell through. It seems that one business was sold to a developer who wanted to build a strip mall. So, he lost that contract. The other client decided to award Alan's contract to the son of a family friend at the last minute. Alan was crushed.

Alan, however, reacted differently. He didn't make excuses. Alan looked at himself and wondered what **he** could have done differently. He thought about how he could prevent this from happening in the future. He was disappointed but determined. He looked into how he could have signed contracts long before the spring. He looked into having clients submitting non-refundable deposits to protect himself. He was determined to make certain that he would have plenty of work scheduled in advance from this point forward.

You see, the unsuccessful always act predictably in the wake of failure. When they fail, they make excuses. They refuse to take responsibility. They blame anything and anyone they can. Then, they quit and refuse to try again. They stay with others who have the same mindset. They cling together and commiserate. They tell each other stories of woe and convince each other that they collectively and individually got a raw deal. They tell themselves that the "Alans" of the world are lucky and get all the breaks. So, they stay right where they are, alone and bitter and feeling sorry for themselves. They wallow in self-pity. (Self-pity is the greatest waste of energy since worry!)

The "Alans" of the world all think alike and act alike as well. When they fail, they take responsibility. They ask themselves, *"What did I do wrong?"* What could I *have done better? What can I do, moving forward, to be more successful?"* They take an honest look at themselves. They assess, they learn, and they grow. Then, they try again!

Successful people always say that *failure leads to success. "Fail your way to the top."* The "Alans" of the world keep trying and failing and trying again until they get where they want to be. There is no mystery. It is not luck. Success is a matter of grit. It is about determination. It is about locking in on your goal and hanging onto that dream like a hungry Pitbull.

The fact of the matter is, successful people just plain out-work the competition. I promise you: You will be as successful as you choose to be. (I will show you how later.) Yes, you will fail. Yes, you will get hurt. Yes, you will be embarrassed and humiliated, and frustrated. But remember why you are doing this.

You set a goal. You decided to go out to get what you want. If you don't get it, someone else will. Jack didn't want it, but Alan did. Alan got knocked down. He got back up and kept moving forward. He failed, he learned, he adapted, and he made his dreams come true.

If you don't take it, someone else will. Why? Why would you let someone else live your dream?? It's your dream! Go out and grab it, and never let it go . . . NO MATTER WHAT!

4.
The World is NOT Falling Apart

Living the life of your dreams can seem like an impossibility sometimes. Life throws a lot at us, and we can often become overwhelmed. Have you ever felt like your life was unmanageable? Do you ever feel like, not just your world but, the entire world around us all is spiraling out of control? If you do have these feelings, I understand. But do not despair. The world is NOT falling apart, and despite how you may feel sometimes, neither are you!

It is important to me that I share my positive message with you. I want you to realize that, not only are you capable of living the life you truly want to live, but that life, in general, is good. There is so much to be thankful for and so much to look forward to, with hope. To be free to reach for your dreams, you need to be free from the fears that the world is coming undone. These fears steal your energy and confidence. It's time to set yourself free.

I want you to use your imagination to create your dreams, not manufacture nightmares. (There is no Boogeyman out there.) You control your dreams. By that I mean, you control the vision you create for your future. You will make this vision your reality. Make this vision something beautiful.

Lately, I have heard a lot of people saying, *"The world is going crazy,"* or, *"Everything is getting worse every day."* I disagree. Things are not as bad as they seem. Why, then, do things sometimes seem so bad?

Things *seem* like they are worse than they really are because we live in such a unique time. There has been an incredible explosion in technology over a very short period, and we have not yet adjusted. We are experiencing a kind of future shock. For years, we relied on one or two sources for our news. The stories came out daily. The daily paper and the evening news reigned supreme. That was all we really had, that, and a few gossipy neighbors. (Yes, I'm old.)

When there was a big story, we would see it on the evening news and then get an update in the paper in the morning. (I got my news by way of pony express.) Nowadays, if something big happens, it comes at us in waves every few minutes. We get instant updates from more sources than we can count.

We can then share each update with everyone we know and our very close, 2,300 fb friends. They will, then, share the story with their 2,300 friends and so on. By the end of the day, we have heard the story so many times that we feel like we can't remember a time when we weren't chatting, tweeting, and *instasomethening* (Huh?) the details (and our opinions) of this story.

What makes things worse, the stories are always negative. The media provides a never-ending supply of unsettling information. They dig and dig and dig for it. When they find it, or it just jumps out at them, they highlight these negative stories. They get it out for consumption as quickly as possible. They have to. This is the world of instant information, and it is very competitive. Once they have you, they can't afford to let you go so, they dig into each story and cover every dirty angle they can find.

This is not to disparage the media. They are doing their jobs. They are there to inform the public. They also need to be able to compete in the free market. If they cannot grab and keep your attention, the advertising dollars go elsewhere. They don't want that to happen. So, what do they do? They supply headlines that you cannot ignore. What grabs our attention? We cannot ignore, tragedy, crime, violence, etc.

Let's be honest here, *"Nice family finds good homes for puppies,"* or *"Students raise money for the homeless,"* are not the kind of headlines that get everyone at work IM'ing each other all afternoon. Once they have you, they need to keep feeding you, or you will go somewhere else for your info fix. The media are just following the first rule of economics - supply and demand. They supply what we demand.

Now you can see why there are so many of these unsettling stories in the media. But in a world with 7.5 billion people in it, (at the time of this book's publishing) the number of negative stories could be far, far worse, that is if we, the people, really are all that bad. I believe we are NOT bad.

If people were actually bad, with the number of people walking around and the intense coverage of, well, everything, we would see far more negative stories. That's why when something bad happens, we see it over and over and from every angle possible. If there was something new to move on to, the media would be in a race to jump on *that* story and cover every angle. But that is not what happens - is it? No. The media clings to a story and milks it for everything it's worth and tries to drag it forward to the next story.

The media also know how to push our buttons. They know what stories will divide us, and they play on this as well. Whenever a politician or celebrity says or does anything remotely interesting, we all get the dirt. (I'm playing fast and loose with the term interesting here.)

This instant information also contributes to bringing out the worst in US, and this pleases the media greatly. They will make sure that they cover every story from one perspective or the other specifically to get us to pick sides. The friction created among citizens creates more stories.

People with different views start commenting on each story. Each comment is monitored and responded to favorably or unfavorably. Then, that comment gets a long line of comments, and before you know it, 100 people who have never met or communicated before are calling each other names. I know you have seen this. You may even engage. If so, does it make you feel better or worse?

We live in a world of participation trophies. We no longer allow kids to keep score in sports, and there are no winners and no losers. However, people still seem obsessed with winning. The winner is the one with the most likes on social media. Maybe we should go back to keeping score and making kids *earn* trophies. That's the way it was when I was a kid. I guess I got all that out of my system.

My point is, this new era of technology, and instant sharing of information will simply take some getting used to, like parties at college. Freshman students often have a tough time in their first semester. They get distracted, have difficulty budgeting their time, and then there's the parties. Oh boy . . . the parties. Young students need to adjust to their new lifestyle, and we must learn to adjust to our changing world.

When social media came around, we started out just having some fun. We were building farms and throwing sheep at each other. (I still can't figure that one out.) Things changed fast, and we suddenly found ourselves devouring and creating content. Now, things are broken, and we are experiencing a hangover, just like a freshman. (Never again, I said, never again.) We need to learn to party (post) responsibly.

Now that we see how the media plays a role in our negative perception, we need to now accept responsibility for our own actions. If we allow ourselves to get too caught up in who's right and who's wrong, because of their opinions and beliefs, we can start down a very ugly path. This will do nothing but cause us stress. It divides us. That is never good.

We need to come together to make things better for all. Take another look at those negative news stories again for a moment. Let's think about what is happening. They usually begin the same way. One bad person, with some ugly ideas, does something terrible. The news reports it. The story spreads.

The story is truly the pebble dropped into the pond. The ripples begin to work their way to shore. The story spreads because it is horrible and scary. It gets shared and talked about, and analyzed. This gives the story, and the ugliness, power. We, as citizens, get ahold of it and give it more power through social media.

We each share opinions of why this terrible thing happened. We have a need to assign blame. Somehow, having somewhere to place blame, comforts us. This way, we can create a call to action. Now we can demand change. There! That will solve the problem. This gives us a sense of control. Control is comforting. Chaos is not.

We point fingers in one direction or another. Then, our friends say, *"Wait a minute. That's not fair!"* and point in another direction. We all pick sides and defend and attack. We become tribal. We dig in, and new arguments split off in all manner of directions. It becomes madness. Because this pattern keeps occurring, and we can't seem to break it, it seems that so many terrible things are constantly happening.

When we consider how easily one person, committing one terrible act, one time, can cause the whole country to devolve into a furious rage, then I am compelled to ask a question. Cannot one person do one good thing and cause others to move in a more positive direction? If that can happen, then, what if many people were to each try to do one good thing. Commit an act of kindness, help someone, try to fix something rather than trying to break things. What then?

Is it conceivable that we can turn this thing around? Can we switch our focus to the positive? Can we begin to simply try to see the good rather than seek out and promote the bad? What would happen if we shut out the social media for a little while each day and simply enjoyed the good?

I can tell you from experience that small positives can carry more weight than even big negatives. During stressful times at work, when I felt like I was being pulled in every direction, I would go for a short walk. I cannot tell you what it meant to me to just go outside and walk in the sun. That's it. Just ten minutes in the sun, and I was transformed.

"When we fail to appreciate the simple things in life, we are truly lost."

-Wade Hoover

The world is not falling apart. It is filled with amazing beauty. While it is true that we are often tested, and we do not always pass these tests with flying colors, we still continue to grow. We all have goodness and great strength within us. It is up to each of, us as individuals, to cultivate the good within. We have that power and the opportunity to put that power to use. Being positive, like everything else, is a choice.

Sometimes we, as individuals, feel small. But remember, so is the pebble. You can start a ripple whenever you want. What is it that you care about? What do you want to do? Who can you help? Start asking these questions. The answers will come. You can begin to affect change for the positive anytime you wish.

Think about this. What have you been doing? Have you been on social media? When you are there, what do you do? Look at the past few weeks. What have you liked, shared, and commented on? Were these things positive or negative? Were they uplifting or critical? Think of the patterns you are forming. Which direction do you want to go? Which direction are you headed? You get to choose.

I want you to be happy. I want you to be successful. To achieve these things, you need to be positive. What you put out there comes back to you. If you allow yourself to get tangled up in negativity, that's what your life will be. I have put all that behind me. I won't engage, in that way, any longer. I have no interest in trying to bring others down. I am only interested in lifting others up. Let me tell you, living this way is wonderful.

Not only does it feel great to bring positivity to others, it always seems to come back. It grows. Putting others down comes back to bite people and, in the end, brings them down. Trying to lift others up, on the other hand is, in itself, an uplifting experience.

"You get back in life ten times what you give."

-Barbara Moyer
(Wade's Mom)

Mom's premise is solid. Things tend to work out that way. I will discuss the law of attraction in a later chapter. For now, I want you to warm up to the idea that your attitude and behavior will affect your life experience.

It is easy to feel the weight of bad things. It is easy to find the failures in ourselves and in others. We are clearly an imperfect species. But we are quite unique in that we can understand our weaknesses, and we can choose to work on them. Most of us do just that.

It is also easy to think that things are hard right now. I have listened to people complain about how hard life is in the modern era. This is merely the perception of someone who did not live through the great depression or World War II. Just for a bit of perspective.

Think about how much easier a job search is now, with the internet. How about completing simple home repairs? I had to replace the toilet paper holder in my bathroom. (I broke the other one. Don't ask.) All I had to do was go online and watch a video. Boom. Done.

These are a few small examples of how daily life is better, but when you consider the advancements in medicine, communication, and travel, we are much better off now. This is an amazing time to be alive.

There are now, and have always been, challenges. Human beings have always found a way to overcome these challenges - to thrive. You can overcome your personal challenges to thrive in your own life. You can get past any difficulties to live the life you want to live. It is entirely up to you.

Don't look at the world as a rough place filled with problems. Try to see it as I now do, as a wonderful place filled with opportunities. The world is what you make of it. You can choose to free yourself from the worries of the world by focusing on its beauty.

5.
The Comfort Zone

You have heard it said, often, and by many - *"You need to get out of your comfort zone."* Be honest. It has probably lost its meaning for you. Maybe it never really had an impact. I would like to change that for you right now.

I want you to truly accept this idea. This is a very important concept, more so than you can probably imagine. I understand that you may nod along and think, *"Yeah, yeah, I get it."* But do you really? Do you really understand how important this is?

I know. I used to nod along and think, "I understand" - when this was said to me. I looked like a bobblehead, nodding along and yet never really taking-in the kind of lessons that could have made a tremendous difference in my life. One day, I tried getting out of my comfort zone. It changed my life.

I'll share with you how getting out of my comfort zone changed my life, but first, I want you to know how *hiding out* in my comfort zone nearly ruined me. I want you to fully understand this concept from all angles. When I look back, I am amazed that I did not see how life was playing out for me and why.

After graduating from college, I thought I had it made. I was ready to go out into the world and build a great career, make money, buy myself a house, and . . . well, you know the drill. I had a degree in telecommunications (now called "digital media"), and I had some experience. I spent a semester writing for television, radio, and magazines. I was all set to live the dream. I thought I could have everything. I thought I was ready to do it all! I was right - on that first part. It was that pesky second part that got me. Was I ready? No, I was not.

After graduation, I set out to begin my career as a copywriter. I wanted to work in marketing, in some capacity. I was never a great student. However, anytime I had a writing assignment for any class, I almost always received an "A."
Now. To be fair, I understand that my technical skills as a writer are not the best. You may have noticed. (Be nice.) But I was usually able to keep the reader interested (Right?) and, I was able to effectively deliver my message. I hope to do that with you.

I was all set to start building a career. I was going to be a copywriter. I was planning on working in marketing and having a job where I could be creative and challenged. This was going to be awesome! Now all I needed was that first job.

I went out and had my résumé professionally created and printed on high-quality paper. This was in 1989. (Internet? What's that?) Not having the internet made things significantly more difficult, but we had no idea. So, I began to apply for positions as a writer.

I had little luck. Which is to say, I never heard back from anyone. When I tried to follow up with a phone call, I was told that I needed 3 to 5 years of experience. I heard that everywhere. *"But I just graduated. How do I get the experience?"* No one seemed to have that answer. I needed a job. I had no money. Things did not look promising. What was I going to do? What I did, was the worst thing possible.

During summer breaks, while attending college, I worked in a warehouse, packing boxes. I used to tell my fellow students that, during summer break, I made money as a professional boxer. (I'm a little different.) Anyway, after working in this warehouse for so many summers, I got used to that routine. It became . . . comfortable.

When I didn't know what to do, I did what most of us do, I retreated (perfect word) to what was familiar. I retreated to my comfort zone. It seemed so reasonable at the time. It usually does. We can talk ourselves into, or out of, just about anything.

While on the surface, making this type of decision seems practical and sensible, it can actually be very destructive. Choosing a non-threatening option to solve a short-term need can quickly and subtly become a dangerous habit. When you create this pattern, it can be very difficult to make progress in any meaningful way. You can end up *"stuck"* in a situation with no idea how you got there or how to get *"unstuck."*

This is where I found myself. I thought to myself, *"Self, you can work here for the next six months, even a year if necessary. Just be patient until you get your chance."* So, I was patient. It just so happens that I didn't work in that warehouse for six months or even a year. I worked there (in my comfort zone) for 15 YEARS! I sincerely hope that scares you.

I hope that scares you and wakes you up to the danger of the comfort zone. You see, the comfort zone lulls you into a false feeling of security. You relax and, when you relax, time tends to go by. You feel comfortable, so you are not motivated to push. When you don't feel that drive to achieve, you simply - do not achieve. Time just slips away.

I let those years slip away because I was comfortable and safe. I was focused on each short-term problem that arose, and I insisted, *"Once I get through this, I'll get back to starting my career."* This was the lie I kept telling myself. I talked myself into believing - the time was just not right. *"Soon,"* I would say, *"Soon I will be ready."* Lies. All lies. These are the lies I told myself so I could hide from change, safe within my comfort zone. Change, however, had other plans for me.

Here is a bit of reality that I learned about change. To live a happy life, you need to consistently move forward and create positive change *on your terms* to make your life more fulfilling. If you do not, you will learn the painful lesson I learned. Either you change on your terms, or change will come to you on *its* terms. When this happens, change will wreck your program in a hurry.

You see, the truth is, the comfort zone is a lie. It seems like an oasis. It seems like a safe place to hide. But, trying to hide from change in your comfort zone, is like a child hiding from a storm by covering their eyes with their hands.

I tried to hide from the real world in my safe, comfortable, non-challenging job. I tried to hide from change. Then, change came for me. Change came in the form of my third, and final layoff from this *"safe"* job. It was my final layoff because the company closed its doors and moved the operation halfway across the country. I was devastated.

Thank God!

It woke me from my seemingly endless slumber.

Look, change is inevitable. Change is also good. Without change, we cannot grow. We cannot become fully developed or live our lives to the fullest. What I am suggesting to you is that you take charge of your life. You should, and can, be in control of your future. You deserve to have all that life has to offer, but a fulfilling life won't come to you. You must go out and get it.

I was afraid to leave my comfort zone and so I never made any progress at all in my life. I merely got older and deeper in debt. It wasn't until I was forced to find a new way, that I was able to progress. What a waste. That can't happen to you. You are meant for more. Please learn from my foolish mistake. You can make things happen for yourself. If you think you are stuck, you don't have to stay that way.

If you are in a position where you don't know what to do, there is something that you can do to find your way. There are steps you can take to make meaningful change in your life. The first thing you need to do is, get out of your comfort zone, just like I got out of mine.

Earlier in this chapter, I told you that I was going to show you how getting out of my comfort zone changed my life. Well, first, you learned that change came for me. It kicked me in the rear-end, and forced me to adapt. That was how I first moved out of my comfort zone. Now, I want you to see how *choosing* to get out of your comfort zone can lead to unexpected rewards. Sometimes, you will find something you didn't even know you wanted.

In my twenties, I was always joking around and, some thought I would be a good stand-up comedian. They were wrong. However, my cousins did convince me to get on stage.

There were a couple of things working against me. First of all, I had no idea *how* to do stand-up comedy. I made people laugh all the time (sometimes on purpose). I was just fooling around and being silly. But, being an actual entertainer? Yikes! Second, I didn't *want* to get on stage. I had *insane* stage-fright. The thought of getting on stage in front of a crowd and trying to make them laugh, terrified me. But I did it.

I did get up on stage, and I did do my stand-up routine. And you know what? I was awful! I went to open mic night at the Comedy Works in Philadelphia. I signed up on a list with all the other comedians who were to perform that night. They never tell you when you will be called up. (That's just mean!)

I was sitting in the audience with my dad, my cousins (who talked me into this nonsense), and my aunts who also thought this was a good idea. We watched one, never to be famous, *"comedian"* after another, get up and struggle. It was a train wreck. I would have felt bad for them if I wasn't so nervous.

After 23 comedians, (I was 24th out of 24 comedians to go up and tarnish the craft of comedy) my turn came . . . sort of.

After comedian #23 stammered through his partially coherent, rambling proof that this was not his calling, the M.C. began to thank the audience for coming out. Everyone began to get up to leave. Now I had to get up and actually *ask* for my turn! I felt like I was asking to be publicly tar-and-feathered. What was I thinking?

The M.C. Said, *"Hang on everyone. We have one more comic to perform."* Everyone stopped and politely ambled back to their seats. No doubt they were as excited in anticipation as I was for my performance. Awesome setup.

Oh my gosh. It was horrifying. I was so stressed before I got on stage that I was sick to my stomach. I was nearly trembling that whole time I was sitting in the audience, and I thought I might trip on my way to the stage because my legs were shaking so badly.

I did the bit that I had planned on doing. It was awkward and uncomfortable. I couldn't see much because of the bright lights in my face, only some polite smiles here and there. I drifted away from my ill-conceived plan and did some off-the-cuff impressions. These were more well-received. Finally, it was over.

I went to talk to my dad, and the manager came over and apologized for making me wait. He said they didn't know me, so they put me on last. He asked if I was coming back next week and told me he would put me on with the first 3 or 4 comics. *"What??"* I thought. *"Wasn't he watching this travesty?"* He actually seemed to think I was OK.

I told the manager I would think about it. I just wanted to leave. I didn't think I was very good, and the stage fright was so bad, I didn't want to put myself through that again. This experience made me *"uncomfortable,"* and I was not used to getting outside of my comfort zone.

I had hidden in my comfort zone for so long, I did not know how to operate outside of my little cocoon. This is a very poor way to live. I wanted to get out of there. I was recoiling from any type of challenge and looking for a safe place to hide. This behavior can only make us weaker. Can you see how I was forming a pattern? I had created a habit of running away from challenges and hiding. I was running away and hiding from life.

Have you avoided challenges? Have you had opportunities in front of you that you let slip away? If you did, don't dwell on these events. Instead, learn from this behavior. Learn to recognize when you are giving in to fear. Fear is the greatest killer of dreams on Earth. That is why I mention it so often. Never let fear make your decisions for you.

After that night, I did not get on stage again for years. I regret that now. I regret that, not because I think I would have been a good comic, but because doing comedy is the thing I mentioned earlier, that changed my life forever.

Life is funny (funnier than me anyway), and sometimes things happen in mysterious ways to help us. I had done open mic comedy, several times over the years. I was off and on with stand-up. I felt oddly compelled, but I couldn't say why. Now I know. One day the oddest thing happened, and I'll let you decide for yourself what forces were at work. I'm just incredibly grateful those forces exist.

I was walking through my hometown of Doylestown, Pennsylvania, on my way to the library. (By that, I mean happy hour.) Hey, don't judge me until you have finished the book. Anyway, on my way to my favorite happy hour spot, I passed a bar that had entertainment. I had performed there at open mic a few times in the past, to varying levels of success. I hadn't performed there in over a year, maybe a year and a half.

As I was walking by, I thought about doing open mic again - for some reason. As I walked along the alley next to the bar, I wondered if comedy was something I should pursue, or was I just kidding myself. I wasn't sure if I should take a real run at this thing, or simply forget it for good. I continued along the alley for another, oh I'd say, seventy-five feet. I wondered to myself if I should do comedy again. I hadn't been on stage in about 18 months. I hadn't done it or talked about it with anyone, ANYONE, in all that time. Then I walked those seventy-five feet, about twenty seconds passed and then . . .

I reached the end of the alley. As I was about to turn left to continue to the *"library"* ahem . . . I came across a small group of twenty-somethings. One of them stopped and pointed at me. *"The comedian of Doylestown!"* He exclaimed. He turned to his friends and said, *"This guy is so f***ing funny!"* and to me, he said, *"Dude! You are awesome!"*

I'll leave it up to you to decide if that was a sign, but that's how I took it. I had chills running up my spine. OK, I thought, I guess I need to get back on stage. I made some calls and talked my way onto the stage at Club 360 in the Parx Casino in Northeast Philadelphia. Normally you need to send a video to be considered. I didn't have one, but I talked my way in. I was going to make a real run at this . . . I thought.

On the night I performed, I had family and friends fill the seats. I had a bit prepared that I had done three times before. I killed with it twice, and I bombed with it once. These are the best odds I have had with comedy. I was ready. Unfortunately, I was still terrified. My stage fright was killing me. I was waiting my turn with knots in my stomach, my heart pounding, and of course, my usual rubber legs. What a mess.

When my name was called, I walked out on this big, elevated stage. It was a semi-circle, and I looked down at the bar that ran all the way across the front of the stage. I saw the bartender, a man in his late twenties, or early thirties looking up at me with an indifference that bordered on disdain. My image appeared on two huge video screens behind me. (Can video pic up panic?)

I picked up the mic and began my well-memorized set. And do you know what happened *this* time? I had my new attitude, the Universe (I suppose) led me to this point. I was supposed to be here, doing this. I was the comedian of Doylestown, after all! THIS TIME . . . I bombed!

Well now. That seems a little bit anti-climactic, doesn't it? Right about now you're probably asking yourself, *"Self, what was the point of that???"* Wasn't I supposed to be telling you a story about the time getting out of my comfort zone changed my life? HA! I'm so glad you asked! OK. No need for the eye roll. Let me finish the story, and it will make sense.

I did bomb on stage that day. I didn't even get pity laughs from family and friends. That seems kind of cold by the way. But I digress. What happened that day, the thing that changed my life was completely unexpected. As I put the microphone back on the mic stand and began walking off the stage to a polite smattering of applause, I realized the strangest thing. It was gone. The stage fright was gone!

I had just bombed in front of my family and friends. I embarrassed myself publicly in front of all. I must have looked ridiculous. But - something profound occurred. I faced my fears. The worst that could happen, happened, and I was fine. I was disappointed, but I was fine. There was nothing left to fear. I learned, once again, that my fears were bigger than any actual threat.

If there was a guiding hand at work that day as I walked down that alley, it led me to know what I was supposed to do and why. I believe I was supposed to get on that stage one more time. I wasn't meant to be a comic. Comedy was a tool. It was the tool I needed to fix something.

I had stage fright. My whole life, I never wanted to speak in public. I even hated giving book reports in school. This problem needed to be fixed in order for me to move forward in my life. I needed to fix this to live what would later become my dream.

It's interesting how different things can look from various perspectives, isn't it? You could look at this story and say, *well Wade, you failed at comedy*. I can see how it could appear that way. But I choose to look at that day as the time I overcame the fear that stood between me and my new dream, the dream of becoming a motivational speaker and helping people live their dreams.

To this day, it amazes me. I can't believe that the kid who got on stage for the first time with paralyzing stage fright, now finds speaking to crowds to be his single greatest source of joy. Life sure is funny. (Unlike me.)

What I want for you is, for you to look at life from a new perspective. I want you to experience great joy in your life. Someday, hopefully a long time from now, you'll look back on your life and smile. You'll look back and think about how amazing it is that so many of the wonderful surprises life presented to you came from getting outside of your comfort zone. Outside the comfort zone, where you lived your entire, amazing life. Where you lived a life of passion, joy, and wonder. A full life. A life with no regrets.

6.
Success is a Choice

One of the most important things I have learned over the years is that success is a choice. I feel compelled to share this idea at every opportunity. I began the first talk I ever gave to young people with this idea. I told them, *"You will be as successful as you choose to be."* This sounds strange at first, a bit pie-in-the-sky-ish, but it will make sense, once I break it down.

When I tell people that everyone is as successful as they choose to be, I mean that their choices have dictated their current level of success. Their future choices will also dictate how successful they will become moving forward. A student's grades, for example, will be determined by their daily choices.

The student will **choose** to get to class on time. They will **choose** to pay attention in class. They will **choose** to ask questions to keep themselves involved and alert. They will **choose** to do all of their homework and reading assignments. They will **choose** to study hard for all exams, and they will **choose** to ask for help when needed. Or - the student will ***not*** choose to do these things.

Any student, with no extenuating circumstances, who chooses to do the things listed above, will have more success in school and achieve better grades than if they do not do these things. If these tactics do not result in the grades the student wishes to achieve, then that student will need to *choose* to adapt. There is no set rule or path to success. There is, however, always the opportunity to find the right path for the individual. The *commitment* to finding *your* path is also a choice.

I mentor a teen student who was struggling in school. He shared with me the struggles he was having at school and at home. I listened as he described his difficulties. I patiently listened to him explain how his teachers were unreasonable. I listened to him explain how they expected too much. I listened to him describe the ways he tried to get help from his teachers, but *"they just don't listen, or care."* I sat quietly as he explained how difficult and unreasonable his mother was as well. Wow. How was this young man *ever* going to overcome these difficult people?

His tone, expression, and body language, all helped to convey his torture at the hands of his oppressors. I was so struck by this young man's plight that I was about to ask him who he thought might play him in the movie. I liked this student though, and I honestly saw myself in him.

Now, I am a middle-aged white man from the suburbs, and he is an African-American teen from West Philadelphia. I know, you're thinking, two peas-in-a-pod - right? Well, actually, yes. The first time I saw him at the place where I was volunteering, I thought, *"That's me as a teen."* We *are* from different backgrounds, and we look different. (He is tall, and I am short.) But people are people, and our personalities are very similar.

This hyperactive teen was chatty and could not sit still for a second. He is funny and engaging and always has some input during group discussions. He is awesome! You know, like me. (Pat myself on the back much?) So, when I was asked by the facilitator if I would be interested in mentoring this young man, I jumped at the chance! I am so glad I did!

Because I identified with his personality, I knew I would have a good chance to understand his issues, particularly his academic issues. I had plenty of my own at that age. When he described his troubles, I felt like he was reading from a letter of complaint that I would have written when I was in high school. I was the man for this job!

Unfortunately, the day I gave my talk about success being a choice, this young man was not present. We talked about this concept during personal conversations a few times. Then we discussed what choices he could make to get better grades and ease tensions at home. Predictably, there were sticking points in this conversation. Most notably, I needed him to stop fixating on what everyone else was doing wrong. I needed him to take responsibility.

Now, I am not a father. I have no experience in raising a teenager. I do, however, have experience in managing millennials. Many of the young people I managed were working in the corporate world for the first time. Plenty, were still living at home and had very little real-world experience of any kind. Managing this group was an invaluable experience.

The conversations I had, and continue to have with my mentee, are quite similar to the one-on-one conversations that I had with members of my team at work. I want to share this with you because I feel that these themes may seem very familiar to you. I find these situations to be quite common. Think about how you view your struggles. Think about how you feel and respond to others at work or in your home life.

Success is indeed a choice, and it begins with responsibility. When it comes to interpersonal relationships at school, work, or even in your personal life, your attitude toward others can make or break your success in these relationships. Relationships with others can be very valuable and rewarding. Unfortunately, they are often wasted. This is an all-too-common reality. It is a shame, and it doesn't have to be this way. Again, this is a choice.

How were my mentee's relationship issues like those of my team members? More importantly, of what value are these stories to you? This will all make sense, I promise.

My mentee was struggling in school and at home. He felt that the reason for his struggles could be attributed to several factors. He felt that his teachers and mother were too demanding and did not care about what he was going through. He felt that what he was facing was too much for him and that this was unfair. He also felt that he was not smart enough to achieve his goals. (That last part hurt to hear.)

Let's look at his concerns:

- Life is unfair.
- Other people are a problem.
- I am not good enough.

Does any of this sound familiar? Have you seen this attitude before? More importantly, have you ever felt this way? Do you feel this way now? If you do, I understand. I have felt this way too. I felt this way most of my life. It didn't stop until I *decided* it needed to stop. Let me show you how these attitudes showed up at work within my team.

I managed a team of copywriters who wrote websites for small to medium-sized businesses. They had certain production and quality requirements which were measured weekly. When members of my team struggled, I would have to show them their stats. They were able to see the stats for the team and the department, as a whole, in addition to their own numbers. They could see plainly, how they compared with their peers.

When they were not performing well, their comments were what I expected. They responded the way a teen responds to their parents when they are questioned about sub-par grades on their report card.

- "Well, other people had worse numbers. What about them?"
- "Sometimes a job will come through which requires so much more time and research."
- "The sales rep, customer, other department, another writer, other team caused . . ." (enter excuse here)

Basically, they were saying - "It's not fair, and it's not my fault!"

The problem was, the same handful of people were always top performers, and the same handful always struggled. After a few months, the one-offs were no longer valid arguments. No oddities which make things difficult could only come to the same people over and over. There had to be something else going on. Hmm . . . what could be the issue? Who is responsible for these production numbers? It's a mystery.

I'm sure that you can clearly see where the issue lies. Now, as a manager, I did take steps to help each employee with their individual issues. For instance, struggling employees were able to be paired up with high performers to learn more efficient methods. This often worked well. This was only one of the tactics employed. But the determining factor was always the employee's willingness to try something new. It came down to their acceptance of responsibility. These things are choices. Making excuses is a choice, just like accepting responsibility is a choice.

Accepting responsibility was a great help to me in my time in the corporate world. I made it a point to be honest, responsible, and as helpful as possible. If I made a mistake, I never tried to cover it up or shift the blame. I was up-front and honest. I apologized, asked what I could do to correct the situation, and I made sure that I was available to anyone whose job was negatively affected by my error.

This simple approach proved to be more valuable than I could have imagined. People soon saw me as someone who could be trusted. They also knew that I would do all I could for them. This was partly because I liked helping and partly because I was grateful for their understanding when I goofed.

Over time, this led to people throughout the company going out of their way to help me when I needed them. It is also one of the reasons that I was able to move up quickly in the company. Doing the right thing is easy. It has many rewards, and as always, it is a choice.

If you want your life to change, *you* have to change *yourself.* You can't wait for something to happen to make your life better. It's up to you to make things better. The first step is accepting responsibility. Once you realize that *your* success is in *your* hands, you can then begin to do something about it! If you are like the student who deflects their shortcomings and says, *"Some kids did worse."* or like my team members who blamed other departments, your situation will not improve. If you are like my mentee, however, it will!

I asked my mentee to do the things I mentioned at the beginning of this chapter. His grades, attitude, and home life all improved very quickly. I asked him to take responsibility. It was a tough conversation. I just wanted him to try. I wanted him to try something new.

When he attempted to resort to explaining how his teachers wouldn't listen, I told him that they *had* to work with him. I told him that if they refused to meet with him and work with him, that he needed to have his parents contact the school about the teacher's unwillingness to help. I was basically calling his bluff on that one, but I stand by my advice. My goal was to take away any, and all, excuses so that he would have to take responsibility. He did. He took responsibility, and he did improve. I am very proud of him!

This is an ongoing process, and my mentee has more to learn and needs to see the act of taking responsibility, produce results consistently. As this happens, he will become more confident in himself and the idea that he can make the changes necessary to improve his life in so many ways. Once he realizes that he can be successful academically, even after struggling, he will be able to see the possibility of succeeding at other things in his life.

This is a lesson that I began to learn in school. I struggled in the same way that my mentee struggled. I was finally able to overcome my underachieving ways in school. What made me realize that this was all on me and my behavior, was that I struggled from K through 12 and found success in college. Looking back, that really is telling. I struggled during my compulsory education, but I was able to do better in college, despite the increased level of academic demands.

Clearly, school doesn't get easier when you get to college. It becomes more challenging and demanding. However, I was able to get better grades in college than I had ever achieved in the past. The reason for this is simple. I changed my approach. I made the decision to do things differently. I finally realized that there was no one to blame but me if I failed. I chose to continually look for a better approach to studying. I made changes to my routine and my attitude. These were choices, and they made all the difference.

Look at your own life. Think about the things that go well and the things that do not go well for you. When you set out to accomplish something, do you succeed? If you try to do something and you do not meet your set goal, do you fairly and honestly analyze why you did not achieve the desired result? Or, do you make an excuse? If you wish to succeed, you need to be honest with yourself. As we discussed already, a failure is only a learning experience, but you only learn if you assess the failure honestly.

Let's look at this entire process in a way that is common and easy to see clearly. Let's think about New Year's resolutions.

This may bring back painful memories, but it is a perfect way for you to see how these principles play out in your life. I will use the most common resolution, weight loss. Even if this was never one of your resolutions or even a goal of yours, I am willing to bet you know people who can identify with this particular goal.

What I have seen are mistakes, excuses, and failures. I say failures because I have seen so many people make excuses and quit. I hate to see this because I know that if these people were to stick with their efforts, keep working, and learning, that they could reach their goals. They chose to set the goal. Unfortunately, they also chose to give up.

When you decide that you are going to do something, you need to make the decision to see it through. In the case of weight loss, if you chose to set this goal, you must then choose to work at it every day. Choose to put in your best effort. Choose to exercise. Choose to eat healthy foods. Choose to avoid unhealthy foods. And - choose to be strong enough to keep moving forward even if you make a mistake.

Everyone experiences setbacks. No matter what you are trying to achieve, you will have setbacks and stumbles. That's ok. You need to see this as part of the process. Keep failing your way to success! If you miss a day at the gym, you can make it up. If you give in to temptation and eat the wrong thing, don't worry and don't make it worse.

There is a great lesson here. When you make a mistake on your way to a goal, and you slip up and cause a setback, work on fixing it. What you don't want to do is make it out to be bigger than it is or, worse yet, compound the problem. When people on a diet *"fall off the wagon"* and eat one bad meal, they all too often go off of the diet and binge. They say things like, *"Oh well, I guess I'll go back on the diet on Monday."* They give themselves permission to eat whatever they want until Monday - when they will *"get serious."* Great. What if it's Wednesday? You can do a lot of damage before Monday.

When you make a mistake, first - forgive yourself. Then, try to make up for the setback if possible. It happens, and it happens to *everyone*. Accept that, and move forward. Get back to what you were doing correctly, and do your best from this point forward. Honestly, no matter what your situation is at any time, you can choose *that* moment to be your turning point. Any moment can be the beginning. You are always in control. Never forget that. Let's take a look at how you can take control in your life.

I always found it interesting how much I have learned about life by going to the gym. You really can see all of life played out right there. You'll see goal setting, commitment, excuses, successes, and failures, all of it, including overuse of the cellphone. I have learned by observing, and I have learned by doing. If you want to put this whole *"success is a choice"* thing to the test and see for yourself how effective this concept is, I suggest the gym.

The gym is a great place to put the concept of *choosing success* into action for yourself. Not only do you deserve to be happy and successful, but you *need* to be healthy. Adding exercise to your life is a great way to move yourself forward, toward a happier and healthier lifestyle. If you already exercise, good for you. But, even if you do get exercise, I bet you have a new goal you would like to reach. You can now work on that goal.

Here is a challenge for all of you. Choose a fitness goal to achieve over the next month. Don't go overboard. What I mean is, this will be a month-long exercise, a short-term goal, an exercise in exercise! This is just to give you an opportunity to dip your toe in the success-is-a-choice pool. Plus, I believe it is always good to challenge yourself as often as possible. This may also get some of you out of your comfort zone!

All you need to do is pick a small fitness goal to work on over the next month. Pick a goal. Decide what you will do each day to bring you closer to that goal, and keep at it, every day, no matter what. Depending on your needs, it could be a weight loss goal, an endurance goal, or a strength goal. Choose whatever you like. All I want you to do is pick something you want to achieve and work for it consistently for one month - and don't give up.

If the fitness goal is not what you want or need, you can choose anything you like. It could be reading or learning something. It could be fixing or building something. It could even be cleaning or organizing. You simply need to stick with it and choose to reach this goal *no matter what*. I only chose fitness because it is very universal and something so many people struggle with. I want to prove to you that you can overcome previous failures and win!

Once you have decided on your short-term goal. I want you to decide what you will do each day to achieve this goal. Just like the student who wants to succeed in school, you need to decide to do the right things every day. You need to decide to avoid the things you know will keep you from reaching this goal. You need to decide to put in the effort. You need to decide to keep at it even when it gets difficult.

Choose your goal for the month. Make a commitment to achieving the goal. You can handle the one-month commitment. Do this for yourself. See what you can accomplish in one month. This will be a great taste of success. If you go off track, start over and try again. The important thing is to stick to your commitment for one entire month. It doesn't matter which month. The sooner you complete this challenge, the sooner you will see how much power you really have!

In pursuing this short-term goal, you will be learning how to create positive habits. You will become more confident and more positive. Nothing is stopping you from doing the things you want to do except your own beliefs and patterns. You will change these negative patterns. You will stop procrastinating. When asked if I procrastinate, I tell people, *"I always meant to."* (I'm sorry, I couldn't resist.)

If you decide to achieve a goal, I mean *really decide* to do it, you will succeed. To decide to do something is different from *trying* to do something. It is not hoping for or thinking about it. To decide - is a commitment. You are making a commitment to the goal, and you are making a promise to yourself. Do not break that promise. If you can't keep your promise to yourself, what good will you be to anyone else?

This chapter was designed to give you a new perspective on what is possible for you. Hopefully, you can see now how success is a choice.

Keep this in mind anytime you have a goal that you want to accomplish. Think about the daily choices you make. Realize that the power to do what needs to be done is always in your hands. Never allow yourself to put the responsibility for your happiness or success in someone else's hands.

Your life is yours. Your dreams are yours. Make a conscious choice to be successful, and you will be. I believe in you. Believe in yourself. Your success is entirely up to you!

7.
Self-Talk

Is it possible to talk yourself into success? Self-talk is more important and more powerful than we realize. The things we say to ourselves have a tremendous effect on our attitudes and emotions. We have established that our attitudes will be the driving force behind our success (or the lack of), and so we will need to find a way to take control of our attitudes. I had to work hard to make that change, but I was finally able to make it happen. As always, if I can do it, so can you.

I want you to get a true sense of my journey because I believe this will help you feel empowered to make the necessary changes in your life. I want you to be confident in your ability to be what you want to be and to live the way you want to live. Once you see how far I have come and understand the path I took, you will *know* that *you* can do anything *you* choose.

In my previous position, I was a manager, and I was part of a great management team. This team, and our boss, made work a pleasure. Even when we went through tough times, having these people around made a tremendous difference. What I want to share is something one of my fellow managers said to me, *"Wade, you are the most positive person I ever met."* The others agreed. I laughed and asked, *"Would you tell my mother that?"*

I would love for my mother to hear someone say that (at that time anyway) because my wonderful mother had seen so many years where I was, um, let's say, not super-positive.

Full disclosure, I was a miserable (censored word here) for most of my life. I was so negative. I mean, I was unhappy, angry, depressed, and quick to judge. I was always down and expecting the worst. You know how some people see the glass as half full, and some see it as half empty? I looked at the same glass and just assumed that someone was going to spill it on me.

I lived most of my life like that. I never needed to hear the first shoe drop. I lived in a perpetual state of expecting the second shoe to drop. If something bad hadn't happened in a while, I just knew that bad luck was simply biding its time and saving up to really let me have it!

I lived my life in a constant state of waiting for troubles and then finding them. I lived in a world of fear, doubt, and self-pity. I wrote this book to save everyone I can, from living life in this manner. The life I was living was going to have me looking back with regret. You will NOT live that way. You will NOT live a life of regret.

I am now an entrepreneur. I am a motivational speaker who speaks and writes to share a message of positivity. I am happy. Sharing this message gives me more joy than I knew could exist. My work is a passion! It is amazing to me that I, of all people, feel this way. And that is the beauty of it all. The fact that I was able to make this change means that *anyone* can change!

These words may seem hollow without perspective, so I thought I would share a story to illustrate my point. I want you to fully appreciate just how negative I was. This will help you to find the positive power within you. Together, we will set that power free!

I have shared my experience of my time working in the warehouse. I want to share a story from my time there. (I was there for 15 years. I have many stories.) This story, in particular, will illustrate how incredibly negative I was. Whenever I relate this story, I shudder at the state I was in at that time. I seemed to be a truly hopeless case. I wasn't. Neither are you.

I will tell you how these events unfolded, and I swear this is the truth. I am not embellishing this story at all. It really is ridiculous, as was my behavior. My behavior is what makes this story such a great example of my poor attitude at this point in my life.

It was years ago, on a cold and snowy Friday. (I walked 10 miles to work each day, always waist-deep in snow, year-round. It was uphill, both ways.) Just setting the scene. It *was* a snowy, Friday though. On this particular Friday, for some reason, everyone at work was in a bad mood. This was strange for a Friday. What was even more strange, however, was that I was not in a bad mood.

Everyone seemed to be at each other's throats all day. There was a lot of bickering and finger-pointing going on all morning. That wasn't odd for this place in general, but it was . . . *everyone*. Plus, it was Friday. (What's up with that?) So, that's how the entire morning went, on this day.

By noon, everyone was cranky except for me - so far. We were in the small break room having lunch when the lead-man came in and announced that he was leaving for the day. It was his birthday, and he wanted to get a jump on the weekend. Besides, the mood in the building was not very jovial. I didn't blame him for wanting to get out. He left by the end of lunch. This is important for my story. (The plot thickens . . .)

The lead-man left, shortly before lunch ended, and two more people were bickering with each other. I got up from my seat and cleaned up the remnants of my mid-day meal, and started toward the break room door. I distinctly remember thinking to myself, *"Man, everyone is in such a bad mood, except for me."*

As I was completing that thought, I had just stepped off of the concrete break room floor and onto the dark, grey carpeted floor of the office. (We clocked in on a computer in the office.) I literally stopped right where I was. My shoulders sagged. I could feel the energy leave my body. The thought came over me, *"Oh, no. What's it gonna be?"*

You see, I had so conditioned myself that bad things happen to me that, if I dared to relax and feel good, I would be punished. Can you imagine that? Can you imagine being so negative that you would not allow yourself to feel (forget good) *"not bad,"* for even a moment for fear of being punished? That is where I was, psychologically. I hope you don't know what that feels like. If you do, don't worry. You can free yourself of those feelings!

. . . Back to my story. The lead man left during lunch, and it was time to get back to work. Now we were operating at, 100%, equally-bad attitude as I had just joined the ranks of the miserable. I went about my super-rewarding work of pulling orders and packing boxes. Suddenly, I heard a truck backing up to one of the bay doors. There were two, large, overhead bay doors for truck pick-ups and deliveries. There were no windows on these two doors, so I couldn't see which door the driver was backing up to.

I went to the smaller walk-through door to look outside to see which door I needed to open. I looked to the left. OK, bay one. Then I happened to look to the right. That's when I saw it. *"Are you kidding me???"*

Outside, to the right, there were eight supplementary, employee parking spaces. There were seven cars there, including mine. There was one empty space. That is where the lead-man was parked before he left, earlier, during lunch. That was about 20 minutes ago. His car had been parked right next to mine. What had happened, apparently in the 20 minutes since the lead-man left, was a large amount of snow slid from the warehouse roof.

Now, I understand that this is the kind of thing that happens in the winter. I also understand that you cannot really predict when it will happen. I understand that heavy snow will eventually slide off of a sloped roof. However, what happened on this day was amazing. Although the roof is long and straight, and the snow was evenly dispersed across the entire length of the roof, the snow only slid off and fell onto two parking spots. Can you guess which two spots?

Against all odds, the snow only landed on the empty spot, vacated about 20 minutes ago by the lead man, and on my spot. So much ice and snow landed on the hood of my Pontiac Firebird that it crushed the hood of the car. The hood was crushed so badly that the master cylinder shattered, and all of my brake fluid ran out. I had no brakes and could not drive the car home. The good news was that the lead man's car was safe. He apparently left just in the nick of time. Also, the other six cars parked in this line (including the car next to mine) were completely untouched. Unreal.

When I saw the damage, I calmly closed the door and started toward the office. I asked one of the other guys to cover for me and unload this truck. I had to let the boss know that my car had just been crushed. He would need pictures for the insurance company. People all rushed outside to see what I was talking about. They couldn't believe their eyes.

After everyone had moved their cars, they came over and told me they felt bad for my luck. They were surprised at my reaction to this crazy turn of events. You see, I didn't get upset at all. I was completely calm. I showed no reaction of any kind. Everyone was amazed.

They said, *"I can't believe how calm you are. If this happened to me, I'd be losing it!"*

I recall exactly how I responded. *"If it were you, you'd be surprised."* And I went back to work. That was actually how I responded. The odds against only one car being damaged were very small. And the odds that the spot right next to my car being hit with snow, moments after being vacated, made these circumstances even more ridiculous. But I wasn't surprised. I was waiting for something to go wrong.

I was expecting to be punished for not being unhappy for a few minutes. Can you even wrap your mind around how pathetic that is? How dysfunctional did my thinking have to be to actually think that *"the Universe"* would punish me for not maintaining my misery and self-pity, if only for a few hours? I was, quite clearly, damaged.

When I tell this story, I do so with the understanding that there are greater tragedies in the world than my Firebird needing a new hood and master cylinder. Perspective is important, and I realize that many people have far-greater burdens to bear than I. I also realize, there are lessons to be learned throughout life, and they can be taught to us in myriad ways.

You don't have to experience great tragedy or hardship to learn and to teach what you have learned. In fact, the most average among us can often be the most heroic or tragic. To me, wasted talent is as tragic as any sudden loss. A long and healthy life lived without joy is a tragedy.

Your life is important. You only get one. No matter how insignificant you feel it may be, your life has the potential to be a meaningful, contributing asset to the world. You have no idea just how far your actions (or the lack thereof) may reach.

Do not sell yourself short. You are significant, and your life matters. You need, and deserve, to live your life as fully and as happily as possible. Once you begin to realize and accept that you can be happy and successful, you will be amazed at how limitless you truly are. Your limits are all of your own making. They have been created in your own mind.

If you can impose limits on yourself, then it is only logical that you can remove them. Doesn't that make sense? Your mind is amazing, and it can alter the course of your life. Certainly, the decisions you make will have a great deal to do with your life's trajectory, but the attitude that feeds these decisions is where you need to start. You can have all the raw materials and resources at your disposal, to build a house, but you won't get anywhere without the blueprint. You need a place to start. Let's start.

It's time to get into self-talk - the things we tell ourselves (and to no one else) over and over, the things that shape our attitude and our beliefs. If you want to make a change for the better in your life, this is where you must begin. We will get into the "Law of Attraction" in the next chapter. There, we will expand on the idea of self-talk and attitude. Right now, let's focus on your *current* self-talk.

When you consider my story and how I expected and received *"bad luck"* can you see what kind of attitude I had? My attitude was, clearly, very negative. It was negative because I created that negativity. I gave it life. I cultivated it like a farmer with a crop. I continually planted the seeds of doubt.

During a job search, I would tell myself, *"I'm applying for this job, but I guarantee they won't even give me an interview."* I watered the seeds every day with negative thinking. *"See, the one company I applied to hasn't gotten back to me."* Then I would harvest a crop of misery. *"No job. I knew it. Why bother?"* (I had tremendous agricultural skills.)

I was always saying negative things to myself. Whenever something negative happened, I would think, *"That figures. Nothing ever goes right".* When something positive happened, I would think, *"That's a miracle. That's the exception that proves the rule."*

Can you see what I was doing? I was starting out expecting bad luck. I was anticipating it, to protect myself from a letdown. What did I expect was going to happen? I talked myself into bad luck. I invited it with my negative self-talk. I used to get angry with everything. Anytime something went wrong, I flew off the handle. This just magnified every problem. When you make a big deal out of a problem, the problem *seems* bigger.

The more you build up and focus on the bad things, the greater impact these things will have on you not only as individual problems but on your life as a whole. Each bad thing seems bigger as you dwell on it. It will stay with you longer. As this happens, you will tend to minimize the good things and not appreciate them as much.

The good things will seem smaller, less relevant, and their impact will be diminished. The good things will be more easily forgotten, giving you more time to focus on the bad. We will go into this in more detail in the next chapter.

Can you see how this can affect your overall life experience? Focusing on the bad things all the time and dwelling on bad experiences and thoughts will bring you down. This negative self-talk, *"I can't do this, I don't have that, nothing goes right,"* and the grand champion of them all, *"Life sucks!"* becomes a self-fulfilling prophecy. Even if things go right more often than they go wrong, you have become so fixated on the wrong, that you completely miss the good things.

Here's the good news. This pattern is reversible. Even better, it can be done right this very instant! I think we have established that I was very negative, right? I also think we have established that I did that, to myself, with my negative self-talk. Yet, I am now, what most people consider me to be a very positive person.

Now, I will show you how I switched from one to the other. Simply send me a check for $450.00, and you can enroll in my . . . Just kidding! This is simple, and it is free. I already paid for it with my 40 years of misery. The bill has been paid. Now we can all reap the rewards!

The idea is simple, but it requires commitment. Here's is how it worked for me. After hearing people tell me, for years, that I needed to *"Think positive,"* I finally decided to try. The move was quite sudden, and I guess I had just had enough. It actually happened shortly after the snow crushed my car. I think that was the straw that broke the Firebird's back - or something. I just realized that I needed to change.

I was burned-out on misery and failure. I gave negativity a shot. I really committed to it, but it actually didn't pay off very well. I decided to try something new. What did I have to lose?

I thought about something. There is a yin and a yang to the Universe. For every action, there is an equal and opposite reaction. There are two sides to every coin. What goes up, must come down. There is a back and forth and give and take and, wow, I kinda' got carried away there for a bit. I guess you have to take the good with the bad. OK, I'm done now. But I did use this fundamental idea to turn my life around.

I accepted that I need to be accountable for my own happiness and success. I had to accept that I was responsible for my negativity. That's when I realized, if I can be the most negative person I know (and it was my own doing), then I could be the most positive person I know! Duh! How simple is that? But is it truly that simple? Could I simply turn the switch and be positive? Can you?

Normally in life, people will say, well, there is no easy answer. Guess what? This *ain't* one of those times - yall! Ha! Finally! There's an easy answer to a real problem! Folks, I need to tell you the truth. I swear that this is actually the path I took, and remember, I was a super train-wreck. One day, I simply said, *"No more."*

I decided one day that I would no longer give in to negativity. I looked at problems through brand new eyes. I saw that there was always a solution. I realized that life was good. I realized and accepted that I could do what I needed to do to solve my problems. I found that solving problems without freaking out and swearing is much easier. Answers come faster when you focus on solving the problem rather than complaining about it.

Don't get me wrong. I still face challenges, especially when I drive. I look in my rearview mirror and see the driver behind me, not only tailgating me - but texting as well! I am being tested. (Deep breath) As soon as possible, I'll give this person a chance to pass me, and I will be in a better position to call 911 - when they rear-end the next driver they get behind.

One of the best ways to work this new attitude of positivity into your life is to simply take notice of your current self-talk. You do it all the time. You probably did it several times while reading this chapter. Things like *"This guy is a doofus"* or, *"Does this clown really think I'm going to fall for this nonsense?"* Be honest. (Wait, am I being negative thinking you doubt me? Hmm . . .) And yes, I do believe you will accept this. As soon as you try it you will see a difference. The change will come fast. It's amazing.

Pay attention to your self-talk and when you catch yourself being negative, stop yourself. Stop, and correct your negative thoughts. Reverse the thinking. If it takes some practice, that's OK. You are training yourself. You are actually learning a new skill. This skill will change your life, I swear it will!

Do yourself a favor. During this process, take notice of other people and the way they talk. Listen to their words and take notice of their attitudes. Take notice of which people display which kinds of talk and attitudes. I promise you - you will see the patterns right in front of your eyes. Negative talkers live unhappy lives. Positive talkers live happier lives. They simply reverse the cause and effect. Their words become their lives, not the other way around. Check it out. You'll be surprised.

To get started, you can begin by being more patient with others. That was a big one for me. Everywhere I went, I would get agitated with people and get frustrated with them. *"What is this idiot doing? Hey, this is the 15 items or less line, and I can see 18 items in your basket! This is anarchy!!!"*

When these things happen, relax. Accept that this is no big deal. Focus on something positive. Tell yourself - *"This guy is wearing greasy work clothes. He's a working man. I see some cold medicine and chicken noodle soup in his basket. Yeah, I've been there, buddy. Do what you need to do."* Then realize, I feel great. I hope this guy feels better.

I know how silly this sounds. I honestly do, but I have done it, and it really makes a difference. This is one simple example. I now do this all the time. No matter what, if you insist on finding the good in others and be as understanding as possible, your self-talk will become more and more positive. As your self-talk becomes more positive, so too will your outward expression toward others. People will pick up on this, and they will begin to treat you better.

Once you take control of, and improve, your self-talk, you will begin to move more and more in a positive direction. You will begin to not just see that you have the *ability* to take control of your life, but you will start to *feel* that control. You are beginning to take control of your life right now, as you read. You are freeing yourself of negativity. You've come this far. Don't stop now!

8.
The Law of Attraction

The law of attraction - This is a very popular and often discussed topic. I have heard it mentioned by many self-help gurus, celebrities, and entrepreneurs. This concept is very interesting to me, and as I listen to people talk about it, I am always fascinated. I have heard different takes on this. I have heard it praised, and I have heard it mocked.

I tend to see things from a unique perspective. My hope is that sharing my views will provoke meaningful thought. I see great value in so many viewpoints, and I think it's important to learn all we can from each other. The Law of Attraction makes sense to me, yet I see the power in a way that is quite different from how you may have heard it described

From what I have read about the Law of Attraction, it seems to be portrayed as something mystical. It has been shown to be its own force, like a tool to be used to do a job. The job is to bring, to an individual, the things they desire. The premise (from what I have read) *seems* to be, *"Ask the Universe for what you want, and the Universe will provide."* The idea is that if you visualize something. Then it will come to you.

This is how I interpret what I have read. I hope you will forgive me if you feel that I have interpreted this message incorrectly. This is simply the sense I get from all that I have read and heard. Aside from how I see this message presented, I have my own take on the idea of the Law of Attraction. I do think it is extremely valuable. I merely see it from a different viewpoint.

When I think of the Law of Attraction, I too see a tool to be used to achieve goals. However, rather than seeing this as a way to ask the Universe to deliver unto us what we want, I view the Law of Attraction as a way to maintain focus.

To achieve a goal, you need to stay focused on that goal. Distractions can cause you to waste time on things that take you further from your intended goal. I think about how we need to maintain focus on what we want so that we do not get distracted from the task at hand.

When I read about the Law of Attraction, I read about visualization. I like that idea very much. I believe that visualizing what you want, makes the thing you want more tangible. You start to see that thing as yours.

To go through the tough times (and they will come) to get to your intended destination, you need to *believe* that your goal is within your reach. If you can see yourself at the finish line, it seems more real. The more real your goal seems, the more realistic (and possible) your success will seem. You have spectacular power within you. So, visualizing what you want is very important.

What I'm unsure of is, the idea that asking the Universe for something, and visualizing that thing as yours, will make it so. I see these things as important, but I believe this is only part of the equation. To succeed in any endeavor, you will need to do your part. You can ask for something and you can visualize it as yours, but if you don't take action and do the work, it will remain a vision.

How then, do I see the Law of Attraction as valuable and powerful? I do very much believe that the Law of Attraction is amazingly powerful, and I do believe that it will help you succeed. I just see it as a practical, and very effective, tool. You have the power to use this tool to get what you want. You simply need to use it properly to be effective. This is what I have learned to do, and it really works!

If it's not magic, then what is it? How does the Law of Attraction work? Let's assume that, like attracts like. If you continue to think positively, positive things come your way. If you think negatively, then negative things come your way. That's the Law of Attraction - right? That is the premise I will work with here. This actually makes good logical sense.

What you focus on will become your reality. This happens for a reason. In the last chapter, on self-talk, I shared how I was always very negative, and bad things kept coming to me. When I decided to keep positive thoughts and expect good things to happen, then, good things came to me. This is the reality. But why? Why do things happen like this? Is it the Universe? Is it God's will? Is there an unseen force at work here? Maybe. I will address that in the next chapter on faith. For now, let's look at another possibility.

When I was focused on the negative, that's what I got. While that is true, good things happened too. My problem was that I dismissed the good and focused on the bad. Two elements were working against me. When I expected bad things to happen, I was on the lookout for them. When I got them, this reinforced my belief that bad things come to me. I dwelled on these things. This made the bad things a powerful part of my existence. In fact, they *became* my existence.

I created and perpetuated a negative experience. Negativity is what I focused on, so when it came, I made sure to experience it fully. When good things happened, and they did, I marginalized these things. I dismissed them quickly and got back to enjoying my self-pity. This was my life.

That is the first element at work - focus. What you focus on becomes your experience. Does that make sense? For instance, when you have a toothache (Yikes!), you feel miserable. You are in pain, and you can't even enjoy a meal. The pain can take your focus. Your experience is negative. When pain is slight, you can be distracted by other things, and you can focus on good things and be happy. If the pain is extreme, this can be much more difficult. We experience what we focus on.

The second element working against me was my vision. My negative thoughts produced a negative attitude. This attitude would not allow me to see or take advantage of opportunity. When you are in a negative state of mind, it is hard to imagine good things happening. When you lack belief in good things happening, you lose the ability to imagine what is possible. If you can't see possibilities, you will completely miss, or pass up on, opportunities. Your negativity is a self-fulfilling prophecy. *"Why try? It won't work anyway."*

Can you see how refusal to accept good things can cause you to miss opportunities? Let me show you, in practical terms, how this worked in my life. Going back to the chapter on the comfort zone, remember how I gave up too early on my job searches? I gave up because I didn't get results right away, and I began to believe that I would never get a chance to do the kind of work I thought I would enjoy. This thinking led to self-destructive behavior.

I passed-up many opportunities, early on, because I couldn't see their value. There were opportunities, but I didn't capitalize on them. If I were in a positive frame of mind, the kind you get when you trust in *"the Universe"* to bring good things, I would have gone after these opportunities. If I had, and the opportunity paid off, that would have reinforced my belief that the Law of Attraction worked for me. I absolutely know this to be true.

Do you want to know how I know this? Because when I decided to be positive, and accept good things and believe that good things are meant for me, I did take that chance. That is the only reason I applied to the temporary position I mentioned earlier.

When I was in the negative frame of mind, I would never have taken a chance on a temporary position. I would have assumed that I would be unemployed in six months at best. I never would have been hired as a copywriter for that three to six-month stint. I never would have been made a full-time employee. I never would have become a manager and had the opportunity to work with some of the finest people I have ever met. I would have remained miserable. Hmm, interesting. I never would have had the *opportunity* to work with the finest people -very interesting indeed.

What was it that led to that opportunity? Was it luck? Was it the Universe? Or, was it getting out of my comfort zone and taking a chance that something good may happen?

I needed no more proof of the Law of Attraction. It worked. I could see that. It's just that the way it worked was different (in my mind) than the way I have seen it presented. I decided to be positive. I began to think, feel, act, and expect positive, and that's what I got in return. But I think the forces at work had more to do with the fact that I was more accepting of possibilities. I became open to opportunities. I started to believe in myself and the idea that I could finally create the life I wanted.

I really do believe in the Law of Attraction. I believe, if you are a positive person, good things will come to you. If you are open to opportunities, you will see them. If you believe that taking a risk, to achieve your goals, will yield a positive result, you will take more risks.

If you take more risks, you will have more successes. These successes will lead to more positive thinking. When you think positively, you see the positive, and good things will come from this behavior. You will be more aggressive in taking meaningful action. This will bring positive and meaningful progress to your life.

Not only will you be able to do great things on your own, but your positive energy will draw like-minded people to you. You will find yourself spending less time with negative people and more time with positive people. These people may become assets in the pursuit of your goals, and you may become assets for them as well. They will think to themselves, *"This Law of Attraction really works! This new friend has really helped me to . . ."* Won't it feel great to be a positive force for others? (Spoiler alert, YES!)

The great thing about the Law of Attraction is that this law works *for* you. You control its effect on your life. You can use it to bring you friends, fun, success, money, whatever you want. I don't think it is supernatural. I think it's logical and sensible but very, very powerful. The good and the bad are always there. Using the Law of Attraction will give you the power to decide which will govern your life. Hear no evil, see no evil, speak no evil, and you will experience no evil. How does *that* sound?

My understanding of this law, as I have shared with you today, is relatively new to me. I didn't realize how profoundly this had affected me in the past. Once I became aware of this law, I began to put it to use. I am now seeing the effects, I just mentioned, in my own life. This is an ongoing process for me. I am in a constant state of discovery these days. My life is exploding with opportunities, challenges, and wonderful new experiences. I love sharing when I find something great. I want you to know the joy that I now feel.

Give this a try. Go about it as others have, and ask the Universe for what you want. Keep your goal in mind. Keep asking for it, and keep your eyes open. The opportunities you seek are there. Let them in! The more you ask for your dream, the more you will think about it. The more you think about what you want, the more you will want it. Keep it always, at the forefront of your mind. That way, you won't miss the next opportunity to move closer to your goal.

If you remain positive, and believe in the Law of Attraction, you will be willing to act on your next opportunity. Action is the key. To succeed in the pursuit of your dream, you will need to act. No one will hand it to you. However, if you maintain positivity, you will attract positive people, and they may be instrumental in moving you forward toward your goals. They will be there for you, especially if you are there for them.

You can do what you want to do with your life. You can be what you want to be. Use the Law of Attraction to your advantage. There is so much good out there - waiting for you. Attract it to you! It will come when you begin to draw it forth. Be the center of gravity for all good things. Your positivity will attract positivity. I really believe that.

The Law of Attraction works for me. Is it really just logical, or is there something more here? Is there a force at work (the Universe)? I'm not sure exactly *how* it works, I'm just so happy that it does! Let's go into that in the next chapter.

9.
Faith

When you set meaningful goals for yourself, you will need to be prepared. You will need to research what steps you must take to reach your goal. You will need to learn new skills. You will need to find out how others may have achieved the goal you have set. You will need the proper mindset. You will, of course, need the proper attitude and the self-talk discussed earlier. And, you will need one more very important element, you will need - faith.

I have a great deal of interest in this subject. For many, it is a difficult subject to broach. Many people have strong feelings about their personal faith and the faiths of others. I realize that each person who reads this book will take something different from this chapter. My sincerest hope is that each of you will give me a chance to offer what I have to share on this topic. I will share my true feelings, and I believe you will get something valuable from this chapter. What I will not do, is push an agenda on anyone. I care about all of you. Every one of you deserves to live the life you want, and each of you *can* live the life of your choosing.

This chapter is not about religion. It is not even about God, although I will share my thoughts on God with you. This chapter is about *your* faith. You do not have to believe in a supernatural being to have faith. You can have faith in, as many say, *the Universe*. This is the faith that there is an energy that guides things and keeps a balance and an order of fairness. That may be your faith. Your faith may be in God. No matter the name you call God, or how you worship, you can surely have faith. You may believe in neither. That's OK. You can still have faith, and you *must*, to make your dreams come true.

When I say you must have faith, it may or may not, be the faith in a higher power. That may be from where you draw your strength, and it may not. But - you absolutely must have faith in *yourself*. You must believe in your chosen path and that you will reach your set goal no matter what. If you do not truly believe that you will *somehow* make it, then you will not.

Why do you need such strong faith? You need this power of belief because you will be tested. I have read, and studied, and researched, and listened to many stories of success. There is *always* one common thread in each story. No success comes easily. I will make you two promises. The first promise is, you will be tested.

Everyone will be tested. You will come to a point (maybe many times) where all seems hopeless. You will need faith to pull you through. Without faith, the hard times will break you. What will keep you going when you are out of money and the rent is due? How will you bounce back from multiple failures? Where will your energy come from when you have nowhere to turn and no one to help you?

When life has driven you to your knees and tears are rolling down your face, and you feel alone, what will you use to support yourself so that you may rise again? You may get to the point where your last remaining asset is faith. Your faith is your belief that you can get through anything because you have decided on your destiny, and you will not be denied! Unlike money, tools, credit, and even friends, your faith will never run out. It is a perpetual asset. It will only run out if you let it. The choice is yours.

The second promise I will make is this - if you have faith, you *will* get through those tough times. Hard times are nothing more than tests. These tests weed out the weak and strengthen those who have the guts to keep moving forward when others quit. Being tested is a good thing. That is hard to imagine when you are going through the struggle, but once you overcome a challenge, you are wiser and stronger. This will prepare you for the next challenge.

Life is always going to throw challenges at you. I like to tell people that, *"Life throws at us both challenges and opportunities, often they are one-and-the-same."* When you are challenged you have a choice - step up, and do what is necessary, or give up. You can just give up on your dream if it gets tough.

Giving up is what those without faith do under tough circumstances. They quit and find an easier (and usually less rewarding) path. They never experience the satisfaction of overcoming the challenge. They never reap the rewards of succeeding at a difficult task. They do not grow and gain strength. Without that newfound strength and experience, they will quit again when things get tough. This is why I believe that your challenges are actually opportunities. They are opportunities to grow.

Do you know what happens to those without faith? When people do not have faith in themselves, they hide from challenges. They stop trying new things.

They live a lesser life. In the end, when you look back and fondly remember all the excitement, successes, and amazing adventures that filled your life, the quitters will be looking back with regret. They will always wonder what they could have done if they just hadn't quit.

If you have a dream and you believe in yourself, you will fight to overcome every obstacle, and you will not be dissuaded by any failure. Each time you stumble, you will rise. Each time you rise, you will rise stronger. What is truly interesting is how these experiences ready you for more than just your current task. They will leave you altered and improved. You will be better prepared to shoot for new goals and aspire to new and even bigger dreams.

Over a lifetime, people grow and change. The goal you have now may change and look very different in the future. Circumstances may open up new and unexpected opportunities for you, causing you to set a new goal. Even if you abandon your original goal to pursue a new goal, the effort you put in and the lessons you have learned will serve you well. The next time you set a goal, you will not be starting at square one. You will be stronger and wiser at that point. Let me show you what I mean. I will share with you the dream I had before I decided to devote my life to helping others through motivational speaking and writing.

When I was four years old, I saw the most amazing thing ever. My parents had divorced, and my mother and I were living at my grandparent's house. On one particular Sunday, my grandfather and my uncles were watching television. What they were watching was spectacular and would alter the course of my life. They were watching football. I believe it was the Philadelphia Eagles (Go birds!) and Washington.

I couldn't believe what I was seeing! The weather was bad. It was raining, and back in 1969, the fields were not as pristine as they are today. It was very muddy. (I was 4-years old. Mud was cool.) I was watching these big guys in these crazy outfits running around in the rain and knocking each other down in the mud. Awesome! Their parents weren't even yelling at them for getting muddy. (Is this for real?) I was mesmerized. I knew only one thing. This is for me!

This was definitely the coolest thing I had ever seen in all my four years! I wanted to do this. I wanted to be one of those guys. I wanted to do what they were doing. I wanted to be like them. I wanted to look like them. They looked so cool! They had on these wild-looking helmets, which looked awesome. I couldn't understand why their shoulders were so big, but that was awesome too. I wanted to look like that.

I ran to my room to see if I could replicate that look. I put on two sweaters to see if that would do the trick. I was too little to see myself in the bedroom mirror.

I ran through the living room past my uncles and out to the driveway, in the rain, to look at myself in the only mirror that I was tall enough to see. I used my grandfather's Pontiac Bonneville driver's side mirror. I was excited to see myself. Did I look like a football player? Um, nope. Hmm . . . not enough sweaters, I guess. Back to my room. I ran past my uncles again. They were engrossed in the game and didn't seem to notice me running back and forth.

I put on another sweater and ran back out to the Bonneville. Nope. This doesn't seem to be the answer. I thought about it for a bit. I went back to the T.V. I looked closely at these gladiators to see if I could see any more details that could help me solve the mystery of the giant shoulders.

Ah, wait a second. There seems to be something other than ten sweaters under their shirts. I later learned that these shirts were called jerseys. (What a weird word.) Anyway, I had an idea - one more try. I made an adjustment and went back to the Bonneville - again. Hmm, this was closer, but I have a feeling that the guys on T.V. didn't have a can of cat food on each shoulder under their jerseys. It was worth a shot.

Anyway, that's where it all began for me. I was four years old when I first fell in love. All I wanted to do from that day forward was play football. I would soon find out that I could play! I could play organized football when I was seven years old. SEVEN??? But I was only four. How many years is that? Three??? I had to wait three years??? But I'm four! When you're four years old, three years is 100 years!

Did you ever notice how your perspective on time changes as you age? When you're four, next week is a far off and unimaginable time, especially if you will get presents on that day. When you turn 45 and realize that you will need to get a colonoscopy at 50, that five years goes by in the blink of an eye. OK. Back to my dream.

So, where am I going with this? What does this have to do with an adult returning to school or starting a business? This story is the setup that will illustrate how your faith can help challenges and struggles prepare you to create the future that will bring you more joy than you can imagine. Not bad, huh?

When I first went out for football, I was seven years old. I was on the 65lb team. The problem, I found, was that I was by far the smallest kid on the team. You see, I am not a big guy. I am only five-feet seven-inches tall. What was a serious problem, for me growing up, was that I was an extraordinarily late bloomer. Not only was I the smallest kid in my grade, but I was smaller than all the kids in the next grade down. As you can imagine, this led to some challenges. Bullies were a terrible issue for me. But that was not the worst part.

All I wanted to do was play football. The unfortunate thing for me, as the smallest player on my team, was that the attribute most coveted by football coaches was size. The larger the player, the more the coaches valued him. This did not bode well for me. I was summarily dismissed by my coaches. Not only football coaches, but baseball coaches shunned me as well. I loved baseball too, but football was my greatest passion. There was a lot of frustration in my youth and a lot of tears.

It was frustrating, each year, having to over-prove my abilities to every new coach. What made things tougher was that I was rarely given a chance to prove what I could do. I was always brushed aside by coaches and told to wait my turn. My turn rarely came, however, as the coaches were primarily focused on the other kids. Many times, these kids were not even all that interested in playing. When we were young, a lot of kids were signed up for sports by their parents simply to give them something to do or even just get them out of the house for a bit. For me, this was everything.

I was just a kid. I only knew what I wanted to do, and I felt like no one would let me do what I loved. I just wanted to be like the other kids. They got to play the game I loved. They were not brushed aside. They got every opportunity, and it meant nothing to them. They were more concerned with getting a free snow cone or soft pretzel after the game. I couldn't figure them out.

I want to share with you, my experience. I believe that my journey is a valuable lesson about how struggle is a meaningful gift. You have had struggles already. You may be struggling right now. Looking at these difficulties from a different perspective may be helpful to you. I raged at my struggles when I was young, and I felt cheated. Now, I look back and see things very differently. I share my struggles and show you how I now believe that they were indeed a blessing.

First, let me help you understand my frustration. Whenever I was at any kind of get-together - picnics, family gatherings, etc. relatives would always ask kids what we wanted to be when we grew up. I always said I wanted to be a football player. The response was *always* the same . . . laughter. Adults, my aunts, and uncles, everyone except my parents would laugh at me. They always had the same comments, *always*, as if they read them in some sort of insult handbook. *"You could run through their legs!"* They would exclaim, or *"You could be the ball!"* (What???) and everyone would laugh. These are "adults" mind you, and I was just a kid. This happened all the way through middle school.

It's always nice to have support when you're growing up. My parents were supportive, of course, and they felt my pain. I knew these kinds of things did not please them. They wanted me to enjoy my life. They were ALWAYS there for me. It is important to have good people around. Family and friends are very important. Remember, support is a two-way street. Always be there for others, and they will be there for you.

So, I'm a little kid who wants to play ball. I am bullied every day in school. My coaches dismiss me and adults laugh at me. I'm off to a promising start, wouldn't you say? Here is the story that truly hits home. This was an important event in my life, during my adolescent development.

In ninth grade, I was four feet, seven inches tall, and I weighed 80 pounds. You just know that the high school coaches were chomping at the bit to get me on the field! That was *ninth grade*, so I don't know how small I was two years earlier on my first day of junior high, but I sure remember that day.

Day one of seventh grade was not my favorite. It was a long day, and I can remember just wanting to go home. In our school district, we went to elementary school from K through 6th-grade. Then we went to junior high from 7th to 9th grade and then on to high school. In 7th-grade, I was in a new school with a lot of new faces. Many of the kids from my 6th-grade class went to other schools in junior high. This was also the first time that students switched classes every hour all day long. This was the fun part. (#sarcasm)

I got a knot in my stomach every time the bell rang to switch classes. I dreaded going into the hallway. When the students poured into the halls to switch classes, I was the immediate focal point of everyone's attention. All-day long I heard things like, *"Oh my God! Look at him! He's so small!"* and *"Do you go to this school?" "He does!!!"* all, day, long.

The first day in a new school is always difficult, especially at that age. But when you are the main focus of the entire student body, and the butt of an endless stream of hurtful comments, the entire day, it can be a rather deflating experience.

Finally, the last period ended. We all returned to our homerooms and waited for our bus numbers to be called, so we could go home. My bus was number 111. I remember that because it's the only thing I wanted to hear. I just wanted to get out of that place. I hated it there. I folded my arms on the desk and put my head down. I wanted to be invisible. I wished no one could see me. *"Please, just get me out of here!"* was all I could think. Unfortunately for me, things were about to get significantly worse. Lucky me. (#sarcasm)

My homeroom teacher, a math teacher named Mr. R. (I will not use his real name), called my name. I looked up.

Mr. R., *"Wade Hoover? Come with me please."*

I thought I was in trouble. Everyone watched, and some whispered to each other as I walked to the front of the room. I was, once again, the center of attention. Mr. R. led me from the room and down the hall. We came to another classroom. I thought maybe I was going to be moved to this homeroom for some reason.

Mr. R. led me into the room and put his arm around my shoulder. This was a 9th-grade homeroom, and I was in 7th-grade. What's going on? I wondered. The teacher, and all the kids, looked at me and probably wondered the same thing.

Mr. R. said, *"Hey Mr. H."* (not his real name, of course) *"I found us a new center for our football team."*

(As it turned out, these two teachers were the school's football coaches.) All of the kids, and the two *"teachers,"* burst out laughing at me.

Mr. R. made me, once again, the unwanted center of attention. He made a joke of me. He ridiculed me, in front of a room full of older students, for his own entertainment. But the worst part of it all was that he did this by using my dream against me. He reached into the very core of my self-doubt and used it as a weapon to attack a 12-year-old kid, a sensitive, insecure kid on his first day in a new school.

What hurt me so badly was that everyone took one look at me and saw one thing. They saw someone who was so unlikely to be able to play football that the idea of my playing was surreal to them. The absurdity of me being able to do the only thing I ever cared about made them laugh out loud.

I have shared a couple of stories of my frustration during my youth. These are the most vivid memories from those years. These events have a way of affecting us deeply, and they tend to stay with us. Experiences of this type can be very frustrating. I remember being mad at God when I was young. I just couldn't understand why things were the way they were.

I distinctly remember asking God, *"Why would you make me like this? Why would you put such an intense passion for something in the one person who was clearly not built to do this particular thing?"*

I, of course, understand that many people face bigger issues. But, as a kid, all I knew was, I was being blocked from having the only thing I wanted. When you have a dream, that passion can be very intense. I am sure you have experienced these feelings before in one way or another. That's why I am sharing what I have learned.

What did I learn from this challenge? I will tell you what I learned, even though it took me many years to fully understand the lesson. Let me first share with you how I responded at this age. This will make what I learned clearer.

Yes. I faced challenges. But I would be damned if those challenges were going to stop me. I was 12 years old, and I was defiant. I was humiliated on that day, but I was not deterred. I was going to play football, and that was that! On my 13th birthday, my father bought me my first set of weights and a weight-lifting bench. Now it's on!

I worked harder at becoming a football player than anything I had ever worked for - until now. I wanted this, and I wanted it badly. I did everything I could think of. I lifted weights. I ate everything that wasn't nailed down. (Who nails down food?) I adjusted my goals as a player, and I kept working.

I had successes, and I had failures. There were times when I quit, temporarily, and then I realized that I had to get after it again. I struggled, but I learned. Over the years, those struggles have given back to me in many ways.

You see, what I learned from my struggles in football is that I could achieve whatever I wanted, as long as I didn't quit. I did play football. I played for many years. I played in high school, college, and even a little bit in a semi-pro league. I played nearly every position on the field at one time or another, including, quarterback, kicker, punter, safety, and - drum roll please . . . **CENTER!**

Take that Mr. R!

The strength gained from these struggles has pulled me through many hard times. Now, it is the force behind my *belief* (and faith) that I will succeed in all my current endeavors. These struggles were a gift. They were the gift that will make me more successful than I would have ever become without them.

Here then, is why I have faith. I have faith in myself. I have this faith because I have been tested. I have been tested and come up short. And I have been tested and succeeded against all odds. I have learned that the only differences between success and failure are attitude and faith. With the right attitude and enough faith, anything is possible!

Now, I told you I would share my thoughts on God. I am a man of my word. I want you to believe in yourself. I will not tell you what to believe in, other than *your* value and hard work. But you deserve to know who I am.

I told you that I was mad at God for making me this way. Now, I am grateful to him for making me this way. I have been blessed with the valuable lessons learned from my struggles. I have been given the gift of vision. I don't mean eyesight. (When I turned 40, my eyes seemed to have told me that *"Anything you wanted to see, you should have looked at already!"* I am wearing glasses as I type. I need new ones.) What I mean by the gift of vision is, I can now see the value in the lessons I have learned. It took a long time, but I get it now, and I get to share these lessons with people who can use what I have learned to their benefit. This brings me more joy than you can imagine.

As for my faith in God, it does not come from church. I have no issues with any church. That's just not where I came upon my faith. My mother taught me about God when I was young, but my faith came later. I began to develop my faith in my teens, and it began to grow.

My faith was born out of gratitude. I had good people around me, and I began to see more good all the time. I did go through a long period of misery in my 20's and 30's, but that was self-inflicted. I merely needed an attitude adjustment.

As I grew older, I turned more and more to God. I prayed, and I changed the way that I prayed. I realized that my approach to prayer was flawed. (Huh?) Yes, I was doing it wrong. At least, that's what I came up with. I kept asking for things. *"Help me with this, please give me that, can you fix this for me?"* Then something occurred to me. I am asking for the wrong things.

I have heard religious people talk about God. They referred to God as *"Our Father."* I then began to think about God as a Father - as a parent. A strange idea came to me. When children want something, they ask their parents to give it to them. But, the parents don't just give them whatever they ask for, even if they can. Why? Because the parents know better, what is good for their children. That's why parents don't let their kids eat candy for dinner.

I have also heard people say that God has a plan for each of us. I thought about that too. What if God were really like a parent? What if He (I refer to God as God, and as He, because this is the vocabulary I have to work with. Please forgive me if I offend anyone. I don't wish to.) actually has a plan for me, and what if it is, truly what is best for me? I may be asking for all the wrong things. Maybe I need to find out what this plan is all about. So, I asked.

Instead of asking God to give me things, or do things for me, I started asking for guidance. WOW! What a difference! When I asked for guidance I got it - immediately. It happened *every* time! I'll share this with you, and you can take it or leave it. I only wish to share my experience. You will find your own way. I believe in you!

When I asked God for guidance, I believe, I received that guidance. Remember how I did stand-up comedy despite my paralyzing stage-fright? I got on stage because, when I asked for guidance, I was led to the stage. Looking back, it was the best thing I had ever done. Getting on stage got me past my stage fright, and if that didn't happen, I don't know what I would be doing now.

How was I led? When I asked for guidance, what happened? Well, I was lying in bed early in the morning before going to work at the warehouse. It wasn't quite time to get up. I was worried about my financial and professional circumstances, and I was very stressed about what to do next. I prayed. I asked only for guidance. Then, my clock radio clicked on. (I set my alarm to turn the radio on to sports talk rather than that loud beep.)

I had just finished asking for guidance when the radio came on, and the sports talk host was introducing a Philadelphia comic. I asked for guidance. My cousins had bugged me to do comedy. My radio came on *seconds* after I asked for guidance at the exact moment a *sports talk* host was introducing a comedian. It seems flimsy, I agree, but still . . . kind of eerie. The thing is, it happened more than once. In fact, it happened many times. I was consistently led toward the same thing. Several times I got chills down my spine.

When I shared the story in the chapter on the comfort zone, as those young folks called me *"The comedian of Doylestown,"* I left out the fact that I had just asked God for guidance, *seconds* before I ran into those kids. There were many other instances like that. I suppose that's what people mean when they say God spoke to me. I could share so many stories like this.

I understand if you are skeptical. That's fine with me. I am not going to try to get you to believe in anything other than your own strength. I am only sharing my journey. I suppose it does not matter from where we draw our strength, as long as we find the strength we need, to live the life we choose.

I wanted to share my thoughts in this chapter. I wanted you to know who I am and how I came to be where I am in my journey. I truly feel that I am being led. I believe that I am supposed to follow this path. I have faith in myself. I have faith in effort, persistence and that hard work pays off. I have faith in God, and I believe that motivating people to follow their dreams is what He wants me to do. With backing like that, how can I fail?

10.
Conquering Fear and Worry

Whatever you hope to achieve in life, you will face obstacles. This is just the natural order of things. Something will always stand in your way, and nothing worthwhile ever comes easily. This is true for everyone, so don't worry too much about that fact. What I do want you to consider is, what obstacles *you* put in *your* way. You need to eliminate these issues before you can effectively take on any of life's other challenges.

The greatest obstacle that most people must overcome is the one that they create for themselves, their own fear. Fear is the greatest roadblock between most of us and true happiness. The fear itself is a tremendous source of anxiety. It can cause persistent worry. It diminishes our daily experience by robbing us of the ability to simply relax and enjoy the day.

How many times have you been somewhere that was meant to be fun, and you spent the entire time worrying about something that *might* happen? Maybe you have a bill that is due, a work issue, or you are having trouble with your job search. Mentally, you were not present. You were at the party, or event, physically but mentally you had placed yourself in a torture chamber of your own creation.

This type of experience is robbing you of your enjoyment of life. You deserve better. There are two things I want you to know. First, you are not alone. That event you were at? Many of the people (sadly, probably most) were torturing themselves as well. Second, this issue is correctable. You have the power to fix this problem. You *can* beat fear. You *must* beat fear if you wish to live your life to the fullest. You can do this, and you *will!*

How can I be so sure that you can overcome your fears to live a better and happier life? Because I have, and folks, let me tell you, that was a battle! It was a rough, long-lasting battle, but I won and so can you. You may have noticed that one of my favorite sayings has become, *"If I can do it, anyone can!"* Why do I say that? I say it because I was so damaged and so lost that I seemed completely hopeless.

I felt as though I was destined to have nothing. I was very much afraid that I was going to end up, alone, freezing to death in the street. I really worried about that. This image would appear in my mind often. It was so vivid it seemed destined to happen. If I didn't do something, it very well may have become my reality. I had to make a change.

What we continually focus on, we tend to create. I needed to change the way I was thinking. I was certain to bring bad experiences because that was all I thought about. My worries never ceased. If I solved one problem, that caused me worry, I would quickly move to another. Rather than realizing that I had just solved a problem, I instead focused on the next problem. If there wasn't one, I anticipated that there would be one soon enough.

Reality was not my problem. My perception was my problem. That was what I needed to fix. Look at that last paragraph.

"If I solved one problem that caused me worry . . ." Notice the important part of the sentence, *"solved one problem."* I focused only on the fact that I had problems. It never occurred to me that I was continually *solving* these problems.

I could have seen myself as an effective problem solver. I could have been confident in knowing that I could handle whatever is thrown at me. Instead, I was focusing on what I considered to be- bad luck. I was allowing myself to be a *victim*. (Yuck. I hate that word!) Have you had worries that consumed you? What happened? You got past them. Even if things went badly, you're still here. Whether you know it or not, you are stronger for the experience.

Many times, I worried about things that never even came to be. I bet you have done this also. Have you filled your head with a bunch of "What ifs"?

What if I can't pay my bills?" "What if I don't get that job?" "What if I mess up this presentation at work?" "What if that international space station falls on my house and Unicorns eat my homework, and . . ." Once we get going on the *what-ifs*, it can bring us to a very unhealthy place.

I was a field goal kicker on my high school football team and during my freshman year in college. I worked extremely hard at my craft. I wanted to be the best. I made sure that I worked on every single detail of my game. I worked on power, distance, accuracy, a quick lift on the ball to prevent the other team from blocking my kick, consistency, everything. I created multiple drills to perfect each element. I improved, and so did my confidence.

In high school when I went onto the field to kick a field goal or an extra point, I had the right attitude. *"Watch this!"* I was focused and confident. In fact, I never considered that I might miss. When I attempted an extra point, I didn't wonder if the ball was going to go through the goalposts. I wondered if I could hit the scoreboard on the other side of the track. This mindset made me very successful.

When I got to college, I was getting closer to the goal I had set as a young boy. Remember, I was going to make it in professional football. I was in college now. Things were beginning to seem real. In fact, I got wind that adults in my hometown were talking about me and they were saying, *"He may actually make it to the pros."* WOW! I couldn't believe that people were saying these kinds of things about me. (I can't resist. One more, *"Take that Mr. R!"*) However, things were changing, including my attitude.

When I was in high school, I was in the early stages of learning my craft and demonstrating my abilities. In college, it was time to progress. This was a new level. Now, I was in a position to start showing what I could do. It was time to make a name for myself. Football was no longer a game. It was getting closer to being a profession, and a young boy's dream realized. There was no room for mistakes. That's what I thought, *"no room for mistakes."*

I had a whole new attitude when I went onto the field. I replaced the *"Watch this,"* attitude, that I had in high school with, *"You can't afford to mess up now."* attitude. What happened, you ask? I messed up, a lot. I was terrible. I couldn't kick the ball through the uprights. I pressed harder, and I played worse. I lost the winner's attitude and replaced it with the fear of failure. My head was always filled with the *"What-ifs."* My thoughts became my reality. I was a train-wreck.

What happened? I was working just as hard as ever, maybe more so. Why was I failing? How could I have been so much better in the past? It didn't make sense. What had changed? Obviously, looking back, the only change was my attitude. Fear won. The fear of failure outweighed my confidence. I lost because I let fear take control. I let go of my dream of playing in the pros. I thought it was over because I wasn't good enough. The problem is, I gave up. I didn't see it through.

What if I hadn't given up? What if I had kept at it. What if I worked through this challenge? You see, the *"What-ifs"* of my past have now left me looking back with a whole new set of *"What-ifs."* The *"What-ifs"* of regret are the worst. Nothing can be done about these. Looking back, I wonder, *"Could I have made it?"* I will never know.

I don't want you to experience these feelings. You don't have to. You won't have to experience these feelings of regret. It won't happen to you, as long as you refuse to give in to fear. It won't happen to you if you never quit. Quitting is the only true failure.

If you have already been through this, as I have, there is something you can do now. You can do what I have done. You can learn from these experiences. Every failure is simply a lesson. It's like taking a class. I have been educated by my failures. I now know that I failed because of my attitude. I allowed negative thinking to overwhelm me and take away my dream. I did that to myself. Now I know that it was *my* doing, and that I could have done things differently. I also learned to accept that I can't go back, but I *can* progress forward.

I use this story to help others see that we all have control over our successes and failures. I now know that even if I am challenged, I will see my commitments through. I won't allow myself to quit again. Win or lose, succeed or fail, I will improve and move forward. As long as I do not quit, there is no *true* failure. I will learn from my *temporary* failures and rejoice in my successes. What I will not do, is create any more regrets!

So, is there a way to get past fear? Is there something each of us can do to train ourselves to stop letting fear infect us? The answer is - yes. There is a simple method to beating fear. You attack it head-on. Face your fears. Seek them out, and confront them every chance you get.

In order to gain a new skill or attribute, you need to train. You need to work on the skill you desire, and you need to do so regularly. Breaking the vice-like grip of fear is not easy. However, it is also not complicated. Do the things that scare you. Face your fears, and you will grow. You will become accustomed to overcoming your fears. You will create new experiences. You will learn about yourself. Most importantly, you will begin to eliminate fear from your life.

You will have challenges, that's for sure. We all have challenges. With your new attitude, these challenges will simply be added to your to-do list and dealt with on your terms. You will solve problems, meet challenges and move on.

That doesn't seem so difficult now, does it? The truth is, it actually is that simple. I say simple, not easy. Fitness is simple. Eat a healthy diet and exercise regularly. See? Simple. However, as the multitude of fitness videos and diets prove, it is not exactly easy. I want to delve into the area of fitness again. It is such a wonderful example to show how our behaviors affect our lives.

When I am at the gym, (and in better shape than I am at the moment), people ask me a lot of questions. The thing is, they know the answers. They just don't like them. They are always hoping that someone will give them an easier way. They don't want to hear about hard work, discipline, and sacrifice. They hope against hope that I will let them in on a little-known secret that lets them eat fried foods and ice cream, lay on the couch, and get six-pack abs. Spoiler alert . . . uh, no.

Getting fit is about forming the proper habits, learning, and dedication, just like success in anything, ANYTHING! Conquering fear is no different. If you keep facing your fears you will get used to it, and life will be easier for you.

You probably have something right now that causes you worry. If this is something you need to address and deal with, then do so as soon as possible. Don't put off the things you dislike. Always do the distasteful first. Get it out of the way and move on, you will be glad you did. If something requires your action and is causing you worry, the longer you put it off, the longer you will have the stress of worry. Get to it now!

If the thing that causes you worry is something that you cannot take action on right now, that is, if there is nothing that ***can*** be done now, then let it go. If there are things you can do to prepare, then do those things immediately. If there is absolutely nothing that you can actively do to deal with the thing that is causing you worry, then why the hell are you allowing it to hurt you?

Let me share a trick I came up with. I used to have a real hard time getting to sleep on Sunday nights. Does this sound familiar? All I could think about was going back to work on Monday. Back to the real world and all the problems that I had effectively put out of my mind on Friday afternoon. I would lay in bed and toss and turn and stress out. I could never seem to get to sleep. I was always exhausted on Monday mornings because I couldn't sleep the night before.

My Sunday-night stress became so bad it would start by mid-day on Sunday. In fact, I began to refer to Sunday as *"pre-Monday"*, or *"Monday eve."* This was a bad idea because it reinforced negativity. This ruined the day for me.

I began to hate Sundays and I didn't want to schedule fun things on Sunday because I knew I couldn't fully enjoy the day. How sad is that? So, clearly I had to change something. Let me first share my trick for getting to sleep on Sunday nights. I know you won't believe me before you try it, but it really worked for me.

One Sunday night, I was having a particularly tough time. I was stressing about an issue at work. I couldn't get to sleep, and my anxiety was giving me a headache. Stress can manifest itself in physical ways. It can make you sick, so you must try to eliminate it from your life. I hope I didn't just give you something else to worry about!

On this particular night, I had had enough. I was tired of feeling like this. I made a decision. I decided to *give myself permission* to let it go. I realized that it was ridiculous to stew in stress and worry over something that could not be addressed right now. I'm in bed. I am not at work. If I go there now, the doors will be locked and there will be no one to talk with about this issue. What the heck am I losing sleep for?

I simply decided that *"I can't do anything about this from bed. I have no choice but to deal with work issues at work. It's OK to let it go and go to sleep."* And I did. You see, what was keeping me awake was the guilt I was feeling about not working on the issue. I felt like I needed to do something. When I finally accepted that there was nothing I could do, I was able to let go. Over time, I was able to do this when I was losing sleep due to worry.

This simple trick worked for me, and I was a real mess. It sounds too simple, but it works. It works because letting go is logical. You need permission to let go. The only one who can give you that permission is you. If there is nothing you can do, then worrying is not solving the problem. Worrying only creates problems. Drop the worry. Get the sleep you need, and you will be better equipped to solve your problems. I would never tell you to do this if it hadn't already worked for me.

When I look back on this, I am amazed at how much power we have. What we focus on and our psychological state can affect us in very powerful ways. And yes, it can definitely affect our health. Long after I learned the trick of letting go of my worries while I was in bed at night, my stress found a new way to manifest itself. Enter . . . the panic attack! (Super.)

I was so stressed at work, that I began to have panic attacks. What made these attacks so scary was, I didn't know what they were. I thought I may have some very serious health concerns. My symptoms varied. Sometimes I would get headaches and I would feel flushed. I would feel a flutter in my chest. That was scary! Sometimes I would lose my balance and my vision would skew. It looked like the world was turning sideways. That was really scary. My mouth would even go numb!

These experiences would come, and they scared me. I tried not to let anyone see what I was going through when it happened at work. I would hold onto, or lean on, a desk and continue a conversation like everything was OK. But I was scared. I didn't know what was happening to me. I didn't know if I was going to drop right there. The fear made the attacks worse. They were brought on by stress and when they hit, my stress skyrocketed. This was very upsetting.

One day, I was listening to sports talk on the radio on my way to work, as usual. I'm from Philly. It's what we do. (#Sportsstress) During the show, one of the on-air personalities was talking about the panic attacks he had experienced. What he described was very familiar to me. Are you kidding me??? I thought. Panic attacks? That's what I'm experiencing? I was at once both relieved and pretty angry. I was mad at myself. I was mad at my weakness.

Here's the part I want you to know. I want you to realize how much control you actually have. You see I was responsible for my panic attacks. I allowed the worry and stress to overwhelm me. I allowed the worry to cause me physical stress. This was crazy to me. This was not going to stand. I am not having it! I refused to let worry control me like that.

The next time I felt those symptoms coming on, I got mad. In my mind, I thought, Hell no! This is not happening! I told myself to knock it off! Don't be ridiculous! Stop this B.S. right now! That was it. The attack stopped, and I calmed down. I haven't had an attack since. I swear to you that is exactly how it went. There is only one small difference. I cleaned up the language for you. I was pretty mad. My language to myself was a bit salty.

Please understand. I don't want you to take chances with your health. If you have experiences like this, please go to your doctor, and find out what is going on.

- Better safe than sorry.

You may be thinking, all of this *"I'm not going to worry,"* stuff sounds good in theory, but come on, how can we believe that we can eliminate worry from our lives? No. I won't say that. I **will** say that you can make significant improvements in your life. You can significantly reduce your worry and stress. You are capable of making changes. It is an ongoing process. At least, it is for me. I have to work at it all the time.

I am dealing with some professional issues right now. That's just the way it is when you run your own business. Your responsibilities never stop. You don't clock out at 5:00 PM, that's for sure! What I am trying to do is, focus on my goals, rather than worry about things that may, or, may not happen down the road. I feel like a quarterback looking down-field.

In football, (Yep, football again.) defensive players try to sack the quarterback. If they can't sack him, they want to hit him as often as possible. Why? Because they want to take away his focus on completing passes and force him to bring his eyes down. In other words, the defense wants the quarterback to look at the defensive linemen who are trying to knock him down. If the quarterback is looking for where the next hit is coming from, he can't see his receivers. He won't complete passes downfield and score.

Can you see how this relates to your experiences? I was a quarterback at one time. (Got that Mr. R? Wow, I really won't let that go.) I understood that I was going to get hit sometimes. However, I still needed to keep my eyes downfield, otherwise the team could not move the ball downfield and we would lose.

I never applied this in my life outside of football, and it cost me. It cost me opportunities because I was always looking for that next hit. Instead of aggressively going after success, I was looking around and wondering what bad thing was going to happen next. (Do you find yourself looking for problems in your life?) Not only was I worried about the next bad thing that may or may not happen, but I was also stuck in a loop.

I was never able to get out of the, *"After I get through this . . ."* loop. Have you ever found yourself stuck in this loop? You have plans to start a business, go back to school, or find a new job, but first, you have to get your bills paid this month. You think, *"Well, maybe after the holidays,"* or *"Once summer is over and the kids are back in school,"* or *"After I get caught up on some of these bills . . ."* I have been there! In fact, I wasted most of my life there. I lost too many years just trying to pay the next bill. You must do all you can to prevent this from happening to you.

If you want to make something happen for you, you must act. You must act today! Do NOT wait. The perfect time will *never* come. If you keep waiting for that perfect day to come, let me tell you what will happen. The day that will come is the day that you realize you are out of time. On that day you will only be able to look back with regret and wonder, *"What if?"*

This is not acceptable. Decide what you want. Bring your eyes up and look downfield and see the opportunities that await you. Be strong. Be confident, and never let fear make a decision for you!

11.
Everyone Pays Their Dues

It has been often said, *"In this world nothing is certain, except death and taxes."* I disagree. Oh, don't get me wrong, I pay my taxes. I also know that I am not immortal. So, I get the whole death and taxes thing. I just want to add a third inevitability, one more thing that cannot be avoided by anyone. I have come to realize that *everyone* must pay their dues.

Taxes must be filed every April, (Delay it all you want, they'll come due.) and death finds us all - eventually. People all seem to accept this. For some, however, the idea that they can escape paying their dues seems possible. It is not.

How often have you put off something you really didn't want to do? Have you put off studying because you didn't *"have time"* or just didn't feel like it? Have you avoided going to the dentist for that sensitivity you feel when you drink something cold? When was the last time you changed your car's oil?

There are many things we avoid because we don't want to deal with the hassle. But we do ourselves no favors by avoiding the unpleasant or the tedious. If you don't stay on top of your studies, you will pay later with poor grades. If you avoid a visit to the dentist because you hate the drill, you will end up with a far more painful experience down the road, especially when you get the bill. (A filling cost less than a crown.) You can change your car's oil every 3-5 thousand miles or, you could be sitting on the side of the road wondering how you will pay for a new engine.

The point is, avoiding things you do not want to deal with does not make them go away. In fact, not dealing with things when they require your attention can often turn small inconveniences into massive problems. Avoiding minor discomfort can lead to tremendous pain. (I need to schedule a dental check-up.)

The examples above show how simple problems, left unattended, can come back to hurt you. This is an important lesson for life. Do the things you know you need to do now, so you won't create troubles for yourself in the future. That's simple enough, right? The sad reality is, too many of us fail to see the big picture when we are young. It's difficult to clearly imagine our adult lives while we are in grade school.

Unfortunately, at this young age, we are already making decisions that will affect our future in very meaningful ways. Failing to learn how to budget your time and be responsible in your youth, can make your adult life more difficult.

When I look at people I have known since high school, who are now adults, I see varying levels of professional and financial success. That is usually going to be the case. Some are doing incredibly well and some are struggling and most are somewhere in the middle. That is to be expected. If I look back and contemplate the actions and choices of these folks, (myself included) our current state is no real surprise. It should have been easily predictable.

I want to address something before I move on, I do not believe in excuses. People love to make excuses. They want to absolve themselves of responsibility for their current condition. If someone is struggling, they will often place the blame elsewhere rather than looking inward.

Placing blame is easier than accepting responsibility, but it won't help your situation any. In fact, refusing to take responsibility for one's own situation causes that person to avoid changing anything. Why change? After all, it's not their fault - right? Wrong! Look, if *you* are not happy with your situation, you must change. If you don't change, your situation won't change.

Let's look at how people end up in in such varied states as adults based on their actions as teens. Think of how your actions and attitudes have led you to your current situation. Now, I do understand extenuating circumstances can occur. Unexpected, major life events can alter one's course. Each life is clearly different. What I want to look at here is, the more typical progression from the teenage years to adulthood and beyond.

I want to share an adaptable concept that can be used to help you make the most of your time and put you on a path to the success and happiness you seek. The first step in making a change for the better, is to understand what does and does not work, and why. You know the answers, but our perception often gets skewed by the experiences of life.

Above I stated that people's situation in adulthood should have been easily predictable. How can that be? No one can predict the future, right? That is correct. No one can predict the future, not even me! (I know, that's hard to believe.) But what *is* predictable is an outcome based on consistent behavior. Let's use a simple example.

Let's say there are identical twin boys, and they are 13 years old. Their names are Bill and Tim. (You may see some parallels in behavior with Alan and Jack, the landscapers.) Bill decides to go out for the track team with a few of his friends. Tim really isn't into sports. He's a good kid and a good student just like Bill, but he prefers to spend his free time on the computer - gaming. He also enjoys potato chips and soda while he is on the computer.

Bill had a tough time during his first week on the track team and realizes that he needs to lose a few pounds and improve his endurance. He begins watching his diet. He avoids the junk food and sodas that he and Tim like so much. He also begins running on his own after dinner while Tim is playing video games and snacking. The twins are beginning to find their own identities. They are choosing their own paths and deciding on their own daily activities.

I suppose you can predict where these two boys will end up by the end of the school year. The behaviors of the two boys will lead them in very different and predictable directions. Bill will have completed his track season. He will have been eating a healthy diet and getting tremendous exercise on a *consistent* basis for several months. Tim will have been living a sedate lifestyle and consuming an unhealthy diet every day over the same timeframe. Although the two share the same genetics and live in the same environment, their physical condition will be very different.

Bill will have a lower body fat percentage than Tim. He will also have greater physical endurance than his gamer brother. This will be the result of the consistent actions of the two boys played out over several months.

What this shows us is, it is not simply genetics or circumstance that contribute to where we will be in the future. We have tremendous say in how happy and successful we will become. What will determine where we will go, will be the decisions we make and what we do on a daily basis.

Bill and Tim's physical condition was easily predictable because their behavior was consistent. Great success in any endeavor is not the result of a handful of massive accomplishments, but rather the daily choices and behaviors that, over time, can create amazing results. Running water cuts through rock not because of its power, but because of its relentless nature. (Boom! Analogy-drop!)

If we look at a real-life example, like the one above, spread over many years, the results will be very similar. The trajectory of the two subjects will be easily predictable. I will share an example from my own life. Oh, how sad this makes me, but I need to face reality. I have no plans on repeating the same behavior over and over. I have changed my behavior in order to achieve a different result. (Spoiler alert - it's working!)

A long, long time ago, I graduated college. As I stated previously, I wasted many years working in the warehouse, and I got nowhere. (I won't put you through my tragic tale again.) During this same timeframe, a friend of mine chose a different path. After he graduated, he found a low paying job that required a great deal of overtime. So, of course this was a salaried job. He was working insane hours without fair compensation . . . in his pay anyway. But, he was very smart.

You see, I was making little money for working 40 hours per week. My friend was making little money for working 50 to 60 hours per week. Without more information, I looked like the smart one. Not true. I had a telecommunications degree and I was working in a warehouse. I was not challenged or growing. I was not learning any new skills that would help me move forward in my field.

My friend had a business degree. He was working in the corporate world. He was learning how business works. He also began going to night school to earn his master's degree. This was a smart move. He was able to get the company he was working for to pay for his school. This was an even smarter move. He was working very hard and making great sacrifices. He was really paying his dues. I was not.

I had very little. I had a small paycheck and few prospects. I needed roommates to afford rent. I wasn't making sacrifices and paying my dues. I was coasting. I was *hoping* for things to get better. My friend was *ensuring* that things would get better. He was being smart. I was being a knucklehead. I recommend my friend's way.

Paying your dues is hard. You need to know that going in. You need to understand that you will have to make sacrifices. You may need to work long hours. You may need to give up hobbies for a while. You will need to get used to sleeping fewer hours. Working this hard and giving up so much for so long seems unfair. Because it is so difficult, many people won't even consider this path.

If you choose this path, you may find that people around you won't understand. They may think you are being foolish. Some will brag about the money they are making or the hot new car they just bought. They may even flash some money around and play the role. Sadly, they may even mock you, probably not to your face, but still . . . Don't listen and don't worry about it. You are in it for the long haul.

My friend's path seemed so tough. His sacrifice seemed never-ending. But, he did get his master's degree (MBA). He did get a better job. He did start making more money. Pretty soon, he was able to do things that many of us could not.

My friend did what so few were willing to do. He truly paid his dues - up-front. He then began to reap the rewards. He has a very nice life now, and he deserves it. He is on the right track and will be able to retire at a young age and still live very well. I am happy to see this because I saw his journey. I made mistakes. I did not pay my dues early and I was not on the right track to retire - but I learned.

We must learn from our mistakes, our struggles and our failures. We must also be able to learn from those around us. I got off to a later start because I did not pay my dues early. I knew I had to pay them, so I got started. Like I said, we all pay our dues. We have no say in that, but we can choose *when* we pay!

My friend chose to pay his dues up front to live the life he wanted. I began paying my dues later. I realized that I wanted more, and that I was capable of more. I finally chose to go after my dreams. I want it all!

I have found my way and although the journey is tough, I now know what I want. I have seen what works, and I have tried what does not work. I continue to learn, and I realized that we all have the ability to choose our path. We have the power to reach our goals.

You can do what you want. You can live the way *you* choose. It is never too late to decide to pay your dues to get what you want. You can choose to do that by the end of this sentence! Did you do it? If not, I will convince you to choose to pay your dues by the end of this book! You deserve to be happy. Pay your dues and you will be!

I told you that we all must pay our dues. I also told you that you can choose when you pay. My friend paid up front and early. I began paying later. Some choose not to pay at all, or so they think.

If you try to avoid paying, the bill collector will come for you one day. What happens to those who decide that they don't want to pay? What happens to those who try to coast all the way through life thinking, *"Hey, I don't need much. It's all good!"* I'll tell you what happens. The bill comes, and their pockets are empty. This is not a bill you can run out on.

What happens is, these folks are left with few choices. None are very attractive. You see these people all the time. They are the ones working at fast food restaurants or department stores when they are in their 80's because their social security is not enough to make ends meet. They are in their golden years. They should be relaxing with their spouses or friends and playing with their grandchildren. Instead, they are being told what to do by their pimply faced teenaged bosses. What is really troubling is, many people have it worse.

This is NOT going to happen to you! You can see the danger ahead. You now understand that your future is in your hands. You *will not* repeat behaviors that have not worked in the past. You are smart. You are strong, and you are ready to pay your dues!

By the time you finish this book, I will make sure you can see what I see. For a long time, all I saw was struggle. My eyes are open, and all I see are possibilities and so many paths to happiness and success. Let's take this journey together. We have everything we need, including, imagination, a great work ethic and a world of possibilities. Let's go get it!

12.
Create a Habit of Success

The habit is truly an amazing thing. Such a small word for such a powerful beast. The power of the habit is unquestioned. Nothing in a person's life can have a more profound effect on the quality of their life than the habit.

Is it possible to control your habits? Moreover, is it possible to make them work for you? Can you use habits as a tool to create the life you want and deserve? (All these questions and more will be answered as you read on!)

The habit can give, and the habit can take. It can be used to create any dream you imagine, or it can destroy all you love. It is a pesky and fickle, little monster, isn't it?

You see, the problem with the habit is, it seems so innocent and even trivial. Often, a habit can go unnoticed, for a while. But eventually, its effect on your life will be undeniable. Nothing is quite so effective at creating massive, life altering change, as the habit.

Bad habits have the power to devastate a life. Good habits however, can help you create the life of your dreams. If we choose to, we can use the habit as a tool for our benefit. Let's take a look at our pal the habit.

Some simple, good habits, like cleaning, dusting and vacuuming will keep our living environment pleasant. Bad habits, like leaving dishes in the sink or dropping dirty clothes on the floor, can lead to a very different home life. These are small things, but they can add up. It's always good to keep an eye out for your habits.

What are some of the things you do daily that make your life better? Do you exercise and eat a healthy diet? Do you keep up with your mail, and most importantly, your bills? What about bad habits? Do you eat fatty foods and drink sugary beverages? Do you snack on chips or cookies late at night? Do you watch too much T.V. or smoke?

These are all common habits, and while seemingly small, they can have a profound effect on your quality of life. Let's look at how you can take control of habits and use them as a tool to achieve goals and shape your life as you choose.

To achieve a set goal, you need to have a plan. You know the old saying; *"If you fail to plan, you plan to fail."* In my experience this has proven to be very true. Here is a simple example that is relatable to most everyone.

Have you ever gone to the grocery store without a shopping list? Remember when you got home and you realized that you had a bunch of things you didn't really need, but the most important thing wasn't there? (Why does that one thing always seem to be toilet paper?) Now you have to go back to the store . . . um, better hurry! No plan equals - *"We have a problem."*

So, the first step to reaching a goal is to create a plan for success. How do you do that? What if you are creating a long-term plan to do something you have never tried before? What if you want a new career? How do you plan for that? What is the first step?

Actually, the first step is to create the plan. Ugh, OK. How? Ah, my pal Google! Thankfully, we live in the information age, and we have instant access to just about anything we need. When you want to achieve a goal, the first thing you can do is research the path.

Let's say that you wanted to become a lawyer. What do you have to do? Go online and search for steps to becoming a lawyer. You will find everything you need. Now, you have a path. Once you have the steps, you can begin working on each step one at a time.

But, what if you pick something that is a little less common, like starting your own motivational speaking business? Go online, and search again! If you want to do something, whether it's huge and obscure, or small and common, you can always find someone who has done what you are trying to do. Where do you think I got my start? No one came to me and offered any help. I had to figure it out. The information you need is everywhere, you simply need to be willing to look for it, and apply what you find.

Find those who are living your dream. Research them. Learn from them. Check out their biographies. See what path they took. Chances are, you will find many examples and many different paths taken. Find someone who is where you want to be, who has come from circumstances as close to yours as possible. They are out there. Learn from them.

Reach out to those who have reached the goal you have set, and ask them for help. Ask for advice. Look for a mentor. Successful people love to share their knowledge. They worked hard to get where they are, and they enjoy passing-on what they have learned. (#Mylife)

Whatever path you choose, there will always be a great deal to learn. You should always be seeking knowledge. Even when you reach your goal, there will always be opportunities to grow. When you get there, remember where you came from, and remember to pass on what you have learned to those who follow. You were once in their shoes.

Now we get to the greatest secret to success you will find anywhere! It's time to learn how to create a habit of success, by creating successful habits. What? That sounds like some double-talk. It is not. What this means is, you will learn how to use successful habits to succeed at short-term goals. As you repeatedly succeed at short-term goals, success will then become a habit. This is very important. It is important because of the psychological effect that this will have on you.

There are always going to be obstacles and stumbles on the way to achieving any goal you set. The important thing to do is, be persistent. The going will get tough, but you must keep going. What will give you the confidence to keep going, even when things seem hopeless, will be your past successes. You will gain a new perspective and a new mindset. When you fail during your journey, you will be able to look at this setback and say, *"I will fix this. I do not fail. I always find a way."*

This is the value of fighting your way through difficult times. Don't forget, your struggles make you stronger. Your new habit of success will continue to give you strength, confidence and belief that nothing will stop you from achieving your set goal. You are a self-made winner.

Using self-created habits as a tool, is the greatest process that I have ever stumbled upon, and it has served me very well. It is the most amazing, simple, and effective tool for success that I have ever found.

The ability to use a habit as a tool was something that I didn't even realize I was learning as a teenager. Back then, I had a habit of lifting weights so that I could compete with bigger kids on the football and baseball fields. It wasn't until much later in life that I realized how to intentionally use this incredible tool to my advantage. It was later still, that I realized that it was not only effective, but completely universal. I could use it for literally ANYTHING!

I always felt that if something sounds too good to be true, it usually (#always) is. So, if you are skeptical, I understand. The only catch (Uh-oh, here it comes.) is that it takes effort over time. It is an effective tool, not magic. But - it IS effective.

I used this tool to get better grades in college when I was struggling. In my 20's, I used it, again, to drop 33lbs. in two-and-a-half months - for boxing. And I used it in my 30's and 40's to get into the best, physical shape of my life. This tool works. Use it wisely and you can do anything.

I will share the story of how I intentionally used habits in my 30's and 40's to get into the best shape of my life. This was the best *physique* I had in my life, anyway. When I was boxing, I was kind of skinny, but I had great endurance. I prefer the physique of my 30's and 40's much more. In fact, I am on my way back to that now. That's a story for another time. Ok, it's, habit time!

When I was 30 years old, I was out of shape. I had gained weight, and I lost energy and endurance. I would breathe heavily after climbing a flight of stairs, and it took a minute for my breathing to return to normal. At 30! What happened to me? The answer is simple, bad habits.

I needed to change things. I joined a local gym. I decided I would go to the gym every Monday, Wednesday and Friday. That's the promise everyone makes with themselves. I was like everyone else who was out of shape, and I acted like it. I made the promise, and I broke it - repeatedly.

It seemed that every day that I was supposed to go to the gym, I would find a reason not to go. I would suddenly feel a cold coming on. *"Oh, I better get home and get some rest. I can't miss work."* Or, *"I think I tweaked something in my back. I better not risk hurting it worse."* Sometimes, I would go home, change into my gym clothes and sit down for *a second* to check out the news. The next thing I know it's 10:30PM. *"Ok, well, I'll get serious tomorrow."* This went on for months! I had to try something different. I did. I created a new habit.

I made a conscious decision to try an experiment. Here was my new plan. (Are you excited yet?? OK. Well, read carefully because this experiment was *incredibly* successful.)

I decided that I was going to go to the gym, straight from work. I noticed that if I went home to change into workout clothes that the gravitational pull of the couch was too strong to resist. It would only let me get as far as the refrigerator. Once I was home, I wasn't going to the gym.

Here is the new plan I came up with. I began brining my workout clothes with me to work each morning, and I changed in the bathroom there. I would go directly to the gym from work to avoid the irresistible pull of the black hole I called a couch.

The second thing I did was also very simple. I decided that I would go to the gym *every day*, Monday through Friday. I was going to go to the gym for one hour each day, after work, no matter what. Once I was there, I was not allowed to leave for one hour. If I was hurt or sick, it didn't matter. I had to go for one hour. I was going to stick to these new rules for two weeks. I wanted to see what happened.

What happened, you ask? I didn't miss a day at the gym for the next 11 years! The only exceptions were if I was too sick to work (very rare) and if I was required to be somewhere else at that time. I was so used to going to the gym after work that, one time, I had a wedding rehearsal to go to, and I turned the wrong way out of the parking lot at work. My car knew to go to the gym, not home, which was the opposite direction. But wait! There's more!

As I became used to my new *"habit"* I began to expand on what I was doing. I began eating much better, and I created a new habit for eating properly. I decided to eat a lean, healthy diet on Monday and Tuesday. On Wednesday, I was allowed a cheat. I could have something I liked. I could have a snack or an entrée that I liked, and then I would eat healthy again on Thursday.

I would allow myself a floating cheat again on the weekend. This way I would eat a much healthier and lower calorie diet, but I wouldn't be in a constant state of denying myself the things I wanted. This made it easier to be really good on the days that I wanted to eat healthier meals.

In addition to the dietary changes, I added more time at the gym. One day, I was talking to someone after my workout. We talked for a while. Then, as I was leaving, I remembered that I had to go to the grocery store. The store was right next to the gym. I did my shopping. By the time I got on the road, it was an hour after my normal workout would have been completed. I had a great drive home because, as it turned out, there was no traffic at that time. I decided to use this to my advantage. I began doing two-hour workouts every day! I avoided the traffic and increased my workout results.

I would do my normal workout, and I would spend the next hour working on things I may have neglected in the past. I added extra training for smaller muscle groups and added new abdominal workouts. This sounds like a lot of time and a lot of work, doesn't it? People though I was crazy.

Here's the cool part. Because I made this a habit, it was *easy*. It no longer felt like work. Going to the gym and working as long as I did, was just part of my day. I didn't have to think about it anymore. That's the whole point.

Once you train yourself to create a habit, you can then let the habit take over! I no longer had *"gym days"* they were just - days. I was so used to going to the gym, I felt like I was doing something wrong by not working out on the weekends. So, I started going to the gym on Saturday mornings. Later, I began going on Sunday's as well.

Want to know the results? I went from 180lbs to 161lbs. I maintained that bodyweight for a decade. I began to gain more muscle, but I was losing fat at the same time. I worked hard, every day. I ate a healthy diet. I did everything I could to be consistent and improve. Guess what people told me. *"Wow. Must be nice. You're lucky that you have a special metabolism."*

How do you like that? Unreal. You see, that's what people who don't want to make the commitment do. It's easier for them to declare your success to be the result of luck, so they don't have to make the same commitment and do the work.

Get used to this kind of behavior. Once you get in the habit of succeeding, people will tell you how lucky you are. Don't get mad. When I hear someone tell me that I'm lucky, all I hear is, *"You made it!"*

This is just one example of how I used habits to improve my life. You can use this method to achieve whatever you want. For instance, I used habits to write this book. Many people say they want to write a book. They have something of value to say, and they want to share it with the world. Far too often their book is never completed, and we all miss out.

Why does this happen? Why do people do this? Because they have the same bad habit that too many others have. It's the same bad habit that I used to have. I recently changed that habit and created a better one. What is the bad habit? The worst thing that most of us do when we get an idea is, we talk ourselves out of taking action.

We come up with a great idea. We get excited about it and talk about it, and then we talk ourselves out of it. Have you ever thought of something you wanted to do, or create, and then immediately began finding reasons why this idea won't work out? Have you done it while reading this book? As you read, I hope you are thinking of great things you want to achieve. I also hope you continue to read so I can convince you to go after your goals.

You and I and everyone else come up with ideas all the time. Very rarely do any of us see these ideas through to fruition because we talk ourselves out of taking action. It is a bad habit. That is the problem.

Here is the solution. Create a new habit. I bet you knew I was going to say that. I hope you knew it! That's the point of this chapter. How do we create a new habit? I solved this particular problem by creating a new two-part rule. This new rule has become a habit for me and I have never been happier or more productive!

Wade's Rule:

Part I: If I come up with an idea, I must take action and begin working on my idea.

Part II: Once I start something, I absolutely must finish what I started, no exceptions.

That's about as simple as you can get. But, just think about how different your life would be if you started this, TODAY! What could you accomplish? What could you build, have, or experience? When you look back on your life to this point, how many things did you intend to do that never came to pass? How does that make you feel? Is this a feeling you want to experience again? If not, then make the simple change. Adopt this simple two-part rule, and find out just how amazing you really are!

That is what I did to get started on this book. Once I had started, I knew I must finish. (And so, I did!) In order to complete this task in a timely manner, I had to create some daily habits. I made sure I wrote every day. I made the decision that I would write one chapter each day. The rule was, I had to start a chapter each day. Once I began work on that chapter, I had to finish it that day.

I had done very well using this method. I wasn't 100%, but pretty close. There were a few days, though not many, where I was very busy with work and after a 12-hour work day, I can become a bit fatigued. Sometimes the energy was not there. I was far better off than I would have been without these rules. After the first three weeks, I had a rough draft of my first ten chapters. Remember, I can't type. That's over 30,000 words via hunt and peck. (Why didn't I take typing in high school?) After five and a half weeks, the first draft was completed.

You need to know that you are capable of great things. There is nothing special about me at all. I am pretty average. But, that's my point. Average is pretty powerful when combined with a dream, a positive attitude, a good plan and the right habits. These are the only tools you need to create the life you want.

13.
To Have More You Must Be More

Everyone wants to have more. Don't you agree? Wouldn't you like to have more? Wouldn't you like to have more success, more time to yourself, more living space, more vacations, a more fit physique, how about, more money? Does this sound good to you? Whatever it is you want more of, I understand. We all want something more, or bigger, or better, that's human nature.

Everyone wants something. Did you ever notice that some people have these things and some people never seem to be able to obtain the things they want? Why is that? We dipped our toe in this pond earlier. I think it's time for a swim!

The reality that we need to face is, while we all have the ability to live the lives we want, nothing will just come to us because we want it. Don't panic. I'm not reversing everything I have just shared with you. I am merely saying that we need to do our part before we can reap the rewards. That's what those who get what they want do on a regular basis. They take action.

Having faith that what you want in your life will be yours is an important first step, but there are more steps. You see, everyone wants something and many people want the thing you are after. It is a competition. You can have what you want, but you must earn it. You can, and you will. The simple fact of the matter is, the one who wants it most will get there first.

The ones who get the things they want are the ones who do what the others won't. You need to decide if you are willing to do more than the others who want what you want. Do you really want it, or do you kind of want it? Others are willing to work long hours. Are you willing to work longer hours than your competition? Others are willing to make sacrifices. Are you willing to make greater sacrifices than your competition?

Like I told you before, life is not complicated, but it is not easy either. If success were easy, everyone would be successful. Success takes hard work. You must be committed to putting in quality work - over time. It will come. The harder you work, the sooner it will come. In order to get more out you need to put more in. If you want your life to change, *you* must change.

The best way to become successful, is to become the best version of yourself. You should always be trying to improve yourself. Think about how you live and what you spend time doing. Are you spending your time wisely? Are you learning anything? Are you improving your physical self? Do you eat a healthy diet? Do you exercise? How many books have you read this week? How about this month, or even this year?

The most successful people read about one book a week. They are always looking to be better and to learn more. They always know what social, technological, or political changes are on the horizon that could affect their business. They are never taken by surprise, and they always seem to know more than their competition.

Those at the top know that knowledge is the ultimate key to success. They have the knowledge, and that's why they are successful. That's why people who are just starting out are always asking more successful people questions. How can I reach more customers? What's the best approach for cold emailing? How can I build a strong contact list? Where do I find . . .?

Well, you get the idea. The most successful people know the answers to these and so many other questions. They didn't know these things when they started out, however. In fact, many of these people were just as lost as you might be now. (I know that feeling!)

It's OK to not know everything. It is not OK to continue without learning. No matter who you are, or how successful you are, you should always be learning. You should always be looking ahead. You need to stay focused and driven to be better tomorrow than you are today. The more you improve yourself, the more you improve your chances for success.

This sounds like a lot. I know, but I want you to remember the chapter on habits. I don't want you to feel overwhelmed at this point. If you haven't been doing the things you should be doing to improve, don't worry, but don't continue to waste time either. The beauty of life is, you can change at any time. You are not a person who fails to improve. You are a person who begins improving right now. You can start right now, and you can make self-improvement the thing you are known for.

Remember how we looked at creating a habit of success by creating successful habits? This is the perfect place to start. You are reading this book to get in the right frame of mind. Finish what you started. Once you finish this book, read another book. Read something that is directly related to the goal you want to accomplish. Set a goal to read for a certain amount of time each day. This will become a new, positive habit. Each time you finish a book, you can add that to your list of successes. You are very quickly creating a *habit* of success, and you are becoming better as you go.

Do the same thing with exercise. Each day you are reading at a specific time and for a specific amount of time. That's great! Subtract that time from any time you used to spend on things that were not helping you to improve or bringing you closer to your goal. Now, add time each day for exercise. Pick whatever you like. Set aside a certain time each day to exercise, and treat that time (and your reading time) as important as your work time. (It's actually MORE important.) This time will also be deducted from your previously wasted time. You have plenty. Be honest. (America's got talented idols dancing with . . . whomever, will have to make do without you.)

These are two incredibly simple habits you can use to create significant self-improvement. You don't have to go overboard and turn your world upside down to start this process, but once you start, never look back! Keep looking for new daily habits to add to your life. Make sure you fill your waking hours with positive action. Don't waste any time.

Important note: Time with loved ones is NOT wasted time. It is the reason for all of this effort. You can work your butt off to make a better life for your family, but remember, they need you. They need you to be *present* for them, not just to provide for them. Many years from now, when you look back on your life, it is true that you will regret the chances you didn't take. However, if you don't spend time with the ones you love, you will regret that even more.

If you are single, and have no kids, get back to work now! (After you call your mother.)

Think of these new habits as small victories. A habit of success means stringing successes together day in and day out. Success is becoming habitual for you. You can find small victories all day long which will help you feel more positive and stronger.

A winning feeling is a strong feeling. It helps you create momentum. I used the small victories method years ago when I returned to the gym to lose weight and get back into shape. I mentioned this earlier, but here is another tool I used to be more successful.

I created these little wins for myself. I was trying to lose body fat, and I created my new diet and exercise routine. During this time, opportunities came up often that would cause many people to lose momentum and slip-up. Have you ever been on a diet and someone brought doughnuts to work? You think, *"Oh, just one won't hurt,"* and 4 doughnuts later you hate yourself. I found a trick to get me past this little problem. I even turned it into a positive.

Whenever someone brought snacks into work, or one of our vendors bought us lunch (usually pizza or fried chicken) I created a small victory for myself. I refused to partake. I looked at it like this, I was trying to get into better shape than everyone else. I knew it would take a while, but I wanted to continue to progress. When these unhealthy foods were brought in for us, what made it easier to abstain was my mental approach.

Instead of feeling like I was missing out, I looked at this as though I was taking another step ahead of everyone else. They were eating badly, and I was abstaining. Later I would go to the gym, and they would go home and eat. I looked at this as a victory. After the food was gone, they were no longer enjoying the sensation of eating. In fact, they were feeling guilty. I was feeling victorious.

While they enjoyed the flavors of these foods, the sensual pleasure of eating is short-lived. The negative feelings, weight-gain, and negative health effects are more lasting. I missed out on the enjoyment of the food, but I began to enjoy watching others scarf down those fatty calories while I ate a lean, healthy meal. It was as effective as doing an additional workout. I was moving closer to my goal. I had fewer calories to burn at the gym tonight.

The point I am making is, everything you do to move you closer to the goal, no matter how seemingly insignificant, is progress. If you can make yourself consciously aware of this progress, it will have a profound psychological effect. You can use these small victories to build enormous confidence.

It is not a handful of huge events that make a success, it's the little things, done every day, that make a massive difference. (It was worth repeating this.) I continue pushing the theme of habits for a reason. They will help you get where you want to go. Take control of them, and use them to your advantage.

Gaining, maintaining and growing these skills make you a better version of yourself.

As you can see, there are many ways you can improve. Keep looking for ways to become your best self. As you continue this exercise, you will become more and more aware of the kinds of improvements that you would like to make. You are transforming into the successful person you were always meant to be. Improvement begets improvement and success begets success. The more you achieve the more you will want to achieve.

I remember people in the gym telling me that they thought I was addicted to working out. I said, *"If you're going to be addicted to something, isn't this a good choice?"* I think so. Now we need to get hooked on success!

Some of the things you can work on while becoming your best self can include other people. One of the greatest joys in life is giving back. Help anyone you can whenever you can. This serves society well, and it will serve you well also.

Helping others is intrinsically good. It is good in and of itself. It is also an uplifting experience. We feel good when we are useful and helpful to others. It gives us a sense of purpose. We all need to be needed. It can be as simple and small as opening a door for someone, or it can be bigger, like getting involved with a charity, (or starting one) and so much in between.

Be the one who cares. Be the one, others can count on. Be the one who says yes when you are needed and never gives the impression that you are being put out when asked. Be this person, and you will be surprised at how others treat you in return. You may not see it right away. Don't bother looking for it, and don't expect it, just trust me when I tell you, the good you do will come back to you. It always does.

Give of yourself and your life will improve. Your days will be more rewarding and your future will be brighter. You are quickly becoming your best self, and you are becoming unstoppable.

You are creating a tremendous positive energy (and you will feel it) which will propel you forward. You are freeing yourself of the bad habits and poor attitudes that have held you back in the past. Keep moving forward.

14.
Naysayers

I feel like I am always telling people two things. First, *"You can accomplish anything,"* and second, *"You will face obstacles."* Both of these statements are equally accurate and equally important. At this point I want to address one of the more obvious and destructive external obstacles you will face. (Remember, it is the internal obstacles that you really need to overcome, and you will!)

The one, universal, external obstacle that everyone with a dream faces, is a group called - naysayers. If you have a dream and set a lofty goal, you can bet that people will be lining up to tell you why you can't reach that goal. These are your naysayers, and everyone has them. I sure do.

When I first said that I was going to be a motivational speaker, a friend of mine made a face of derision and began to say, *"You don't have the credent..."* I cut him off right there. I told him, *"Don't even bother telling my why I can't do this. I am doing it, and I don't care what anyone says. I don't care how hard it will be or how long it will take. This decision has been made and that's that!"* That was a short conversation.

I want you to understand your naysayers so that you can overcome this imaginary obstacle. I say imaginary because, try as they might, they cannot actually stop you. They can only try to convince you to quit, or not start at all. They only have the power *you* give them. You will soon see that you do not have to give them any power at all.

Let's look at who your naysayers are and what motivates them. Once you understand them, their credibility will be gone and you will feel confident to get to work making your dreams come true.

I have identified two separate groups of naysayers. They are very different, and their motives are quite different. Both will try very hard to convince you not to commit to your dreams. They will be very convincing. If they can't prevent you from beginning your journey, they will become increasingly more vocal whenever you hit your inevitable stumbling blocks. They will see any struggle as an opportunity to show you the *"proof"* that you cannot succeed. When you see their *"proof"* they will tell you that you need to quit. Let's take a close look at your naysayers.

The first group of naysayers are your family and friends. They will try to stop you from perusing your dream, which seems mean spirited, but it's not. These are the people who care about you. They will try to stop you from doing something that will cause you pain. They don't want to see you fail. They are trying to protect you. They want you to choose a safe route, an easier route, and a route where there are no risks.

Basically, they are afraid to leave their own comfort zone. They fear the unknown. It is scary and dangerous, and they cannot understand why you would take such chances. They want you to stay where it is safe. Unfortunately, as we now know, hiding in the comfort zone only protects you from success. Also, the safety of the comfort zone is a myth. You must choose to change for your own benefit, or change will come when you least expect it and turn your world upside down. (#Layoffs)

Try to be understanding with *these* naysayers. They mean well. They simply cannot see your dream, because it's not *their* dream. It's your dream! They cannot see your vision of the end goal. They merely fear the pain you will feel when you fail. You will fail, repeatedly. That is a natural part of the process of achieving greatness. You will fail for certain, but you won't quit.

Each time you fail, two things will happen. Your naysayers will try to get you to quit, and you will learn something. Ignore the naysayers, and use what you have learned to move toward your goal. You were meant to fail because you need to learn. You started this journey knowing nothing. By the time you reach your goal you will be amazed at how well your failures have prepared you for success.

Let's take a look at the second type of naysayer. This group is very different from your family and friends. These people are more malicious. These are your contemporaries, the people you go to school or work with. They may be from your neighborhood. These people share a socioeconomic background similar to yours. Sadly, some of these people are your friends. They don't want to protect you from failure. The want to protect themselves from your success! Yes, *your* success.

For this group, there is nothing on earth more threatening than the success of those around them. They fear your success more than your family and friends fear your failure. Why? This phenomenon is simple. You see, if you set out to achieve something big, something that seems out of reach for someone from your environment, and you make it, you have proved it can be done. In this case, you have shattered the false reality that they have created for themselves.

Remember how successful people fail more than the unsuccessful? The reason being that they take more chances and refuse to let their failures deter them. Those who do not succeed, fear failure so much that they quit trying. They make excuses as to why they cannot succeed and they never take chances. Their excuses are always that - some outside force makes it impossible for them. They will not admit that they simply don't have the guts to try. You do, and they don't like that fact.

If you succeed, then what you have done is taken away their excuse. They have told everyone that reaching for a higher goal is foolish because it cannot be done. They say that it is impossible to succeed, and so it makes no sense to try. They choose to believe that this is the case. They don't have your courage, or your heart, and it is so much easier to make excuses than to work hard. (#Lazy)

Why take a risk? Why make sacrifices? Why get up early and work long hours? Why challenge yourself when you can take the easy way out and make up some phony excuse? Now they can sit back, relax and live a lesser life filled with excuses, whining and complaining about how lucky other people are.

When you succeed, after they have made excuses for years, you just took that cozy, security blanket away. Now they stand there, proven wrong and looking weak. They are out of excuses. You have just forced them to look at themselves and accept the reality that they just didn't have your strength. They will never say it out loud. They may even try to lie to themselves.

Publicly, they will say that you got lucky. They will do everything to try to tear down your accomplishments. They will say that you had some special advantage or that you have done something shady. They will try to do themselves credit by saying that they are above doing the kinds of things that you *"probably"* did to get where you are. I have some advice for you for when this happens. Let it go.

When people say these things all they are really saying, (and this is what I choose to hear) is that you have won. You did it. You are a success. They are telling you that they are jealous. They are telling you that they feel inferior to you.

You don't have to address their comments at all. Simply drive your new Mercedes home, park it in your four-car garage, next to the Porsche, and go for a swim in your pool. Isn't that more relaxing than arguing with a jealous fool? (#Winning)

There is no point listening to anything your naysayers have to say. Listening to them can only give you self-doubt. The greatest obstacles you face are within you. Do not let anyone cause you to doubt yourself. Your naysayers are weak. They only have the power *you* give them. Give them none.

15.
Your Three Gifts Make You Unstoppable

It took me a long time to realize that you can do just about anything you choose. I struggled for so many years for so many reasons. I didn't understand what life should be. I didn't understand what I could or should do to live my life fully.

I had so much going for me but, I had no idea of the wonderful gifts that were bestowed upon me. I did not realize what amazing gifts all human beings were given at birth. Once I began to analyze my life, I became aware of some things that had previously eluded me.

I now believe that we are all born with three amazing gifts. Once we understand these three gifts, we can put them to use for our own betterment. The three gifts you were born with can make you an unstoppable machine of achievement. Once you realize the power you have, you will be able to do more than you ever thought possible. All you need to do is use your three gifts. It's really not very complicated.

As usual, like everything I share, these gifts are simple and fundamental. But, do not be fooled, their simplicity does not make them any less powerful. Let's examine these wonderful gifts one by one.

The first gift each of us is born with is the beautiful gift of free will. This is paramount to everything you experience in life. Human beings have the freedom to choose their own path. Your life belongs to you, and you decide what kind of life that will be. You already know that you will be as successful as you choose to be. Not only will you determine your level of success, but you choose the goal you will achieve.

It is entirely up to you to decide what direction to take. Do not undervalue this magnificent gift. No other creature in the history of this planet has ever had this gift. It is uniquely ours. Every other creature depends on instinct for survival.

A bird doesn't build a nest because it thinks it's a good idea. Birds build nests because it is genetically programmed into their DNA to do so. They have absolutely no say in the matter. Human beings, on the other hand, have cognitive reasoning. We decide what we will do and who we will be. Far too often, we take this beautiful gift for granted.

When we decide to follow the pack and take the road most traveled, we should ask ourselves why we are doing this. If you have done this, or are doing this now, ask yourself why. Is this what you really want? Do you find this fulfilling? Are you living the life you truly want, need and deserve to live?

When we take our free will for granted and retreat to the comfort of the familiar, simply because that is what we have been shown, I feel that this is wasteful and tragic. Especially if we are not happy.

Why would you spend your entire life following a path that you do not find fulfilling when you could do something that makes each and every day worthwhile? Why settle for something that does not make you happy? You only have one life, live it to the fullest! Anything less is a terrible waste.

Let's say you are working a job you don't like, and you're making just enough income to get by. You spend your entire life worrying about money, retirement and all the *"What-ifs"* that come with financial struggle. This is a sad way to live. (I am speaking from experience.) But what if there was something better for you? What if you had a better way? That way exists. The better way is to use your *second* gift. This one is a bit more complicated.

Free will is a gift that we all share. The second gift, as I see it, is a little different. Each of us has a gift unique unto ourselves. Each of us has something that is ours and ours alone. This is the gift that makes us who we are as individuals. It is a talent, a skill that comes to us naturally. It is something that we do well without even trying, and it usually brings us joy.

This gift could be anything. It is your unique talent. It could be related to the arts. Maybe you can sing or play musical instruments. Perhaps you can paint. Maybe you enjoy cooking and creating delicious meals. Your talent could be anything. You might have great, natural leadership or organizational skills. Maybe you were born to teach. There is literally no end to the possibilities. The trick is, finding *your* gift, the thing that feeds you.

You may know what your gift is already and you may not. If you do not know what your gift is, you need to find out. I believe with all my heart that you were given your gift for a purpose. Your talent is called a *gift* for a reason. It is important. It was not just given to you to entertain friends and family or make life easier for your boss. You were meant to develop your gift, for yourself, and the world around you. It is your contribution to the world. I truly believe that.

Sometimes we feel small. We can forget what influence we have on others. We contribute to the world far more than we realize. We also get to choose (free will) what we contribute. We can choose to contribute positively or negatively. If we go out of our way to be friendly, polite and helpful, this will definitely affect those around us. If we are disrespectful or rude, we will pass this along as well.

Have you ever been stopped at a traffic light, and when the light turns green, the car in front of you just sits there? The other driver is either texting or just not focused. You want to let them know that the light has changed, so you tap your horn. The driver looks up at the light then, in the rear-view mirror, at you (as if you somehow changed the light) and then gives you the bird before driving off as the light turns red. (Son-of-a . . .!)

How does that affect you? Being treated rudely by a stranger when you have done nothing wrong can make you mad. Now you're driving down the road with a bad attitude. You stop at a convenience store for a coffee before work, still thinking about that knucklehead that flipped you off. You walk in and without realizing it, you let the door swing back in the face of an elderly woman. Now you are the rude one, and anyone that saw that thinks you are a jerk.

This is a simple example, but it illustrates how we can unknowingly affect those around us. One rude driver caused a chain of events that negatively affected the morning routine of, well, who knows how many people? We can have a positive effect as well. Simple acts of kindness can spread a positive attitude in the same way.

Just think, what if you *did* find your gift? What if you developed it so that you could use it to make your life better? What if you could use your gift to make a good living and help others at the same time? Wouldn't that be wonderful?

If it sounds to be too good to be true, I assure you, it is not. People do it every day. There is no reason you cannot be one of those people. Why can't you make a successful career doing something you truly enjoy? We tend to excel at the things we enjoy. You can make a great life doing what you love.

In order to live this fuller and happier life, you need to first find your gift. I had trouble with this. I was looking at things differently, and I did what so many of us do. I tried to make my career out of something that I loved, but which was not my gift. My quest to play football, professionally, helped me in many ways. But it was not my gift. The pursuit of this dream was not wasted time either.

Without my quest for football, I would not have developed the work ethic, the drive, the resilience, or the ability to push through any and all obstacles between myself and my goal. When you put everything you have into your dream, you win. You may not see it right away, but you win.

I didn't understand that when I finally walked away from football. I felt like all my efforts were a waste of time. They were no waste of time. All that I put in; I have received back tenfold, just like my mother always said. Now, I have found my gift and I am living a far better life than I believed I had any right to even wish for. You can have this too. So, let's find your gift.

If I had not done stand-up comedy, I would not have found my gift, my love of speaking. Now, I want you to use what I have learned. I want you to get out of your comfort zone, and try as many new things as you can. Try things that interest you and try things that scare you. Face your fears, and defeat them. Conquer you fears and become stronger. You will not regret it.

Each time you face a fear and overcome it, you will become more and more willing to try new things. This newfound strength will serve you well while you work to achieve your goals. It will also give you more and more opportunity to find your gift. My gift was something completely unexpected, yours may be too. Life is funny and often very surprising.

I want for you to have a life that brings you joy. I want you to be successful and have the abundance you deserve. You need to find your gift and bring it to life. You do not want to leave this beautiful gift behind. It is waiting to serve you. Let it.

Once you find your unique gift, you will be ready to use the third gift to give it life. The third gift we all have is another gift that only human beings share.

This gift is will power. The human will, is the greatest power since the sun. When harnessed, and used to achieve a goal, any goal can be accomplished.

On May 25 1961, President John F. Kennedy announced to congress that an American would land on the moon before the end of the decade. On July 20, 1969, that dream was realized. American astronaut Neil Armstrong became the first person to walk on the moon. This amazing feat was accomplished a mere 66 years after the Wright brothers historic first flight in 1903.

This is an example of the power of the human will. If human beings can construct a craft to take other human beings to the moon, and bring them back safely, what can't be done?

Your will power is incredibly strong. It can save your life. The amazing power of the human will is, in my mind, indomitable. This power is there to pull us through the times we never thought we could get through. It pulls soldiers through combat, patients through recovery and a nation through tragedy. (9/11)

When I think of this power, I wonder. What would happen if we used this power to *serve* us, rather than waiting for it to *save* us? Look at what people have accomplished and you will see.

When people use will to serve them, what do we get? We get a man on the moon. We get the Constitution of the United States of America. We get individual success stories that inspire us. We get Oprah Winfrey, a self-made Billionaire. Oprah was told by T.V. executives that she didn't have what it takes to make it in television. (Good call there.)

We get Michael Jorden, possibly the greatest basketball player of all time. Michael Jorden was cut from his 10th-grade basketball team. (HUH???)

We get Bill Gates and Steve Jobs and a heaping, helping of technology. With their contributions, the world has been changed forever. (Side note, they made a buck or two as well.)

We get Dr. Martin Luther King Jr. and one seriously beautiful dream.

You may be thinking that you have nothing in common with these people, but you're wrong. They were gifted, it's true. But, as you have just read, you have three beautiful gifts of your own. You have the same gifts as theses amazing people. If you don't think you are that strong, let me share this perspective with you.

While giving a talk about will power, I asked a group of millennials a question. I asked:

"How many of you think you could go to an indoor swimming pool today and swim, in ideal conditions, 500 yards? You are not allowed to touch the side of the pool or the bottom."

"The water is 76 degrees, 4 feet deep, and we would be indoors. If you cannot swim, you will have a small floatation device. You would have some time to practice holding onto this device and kicking to propel yourself. You can stand up if you have to, but you will fail the test. There is no time limit. How many of you could do this?"

"Look around." Only a few people had their hands up. *"OK. Let's say that this whole group were on a ship, and it sank 500 yards off shore. How many of you think you could make it to shore? The swimmers have no floatation devices, the non-swimmers do. Raise your hands if you think you could make it."* More hands went up, but not all.

"One more try . . ." I said, *"Imagine you are out at sea. You are in the north Atlantic. It's getting dark, and the air is cold. The water is cold, and you are shivering. This time it is just you in the water. It's just you, and a small, crying child. How many of you would get that child to the beach 500 yards away?"*

Jackpot. *"Look around now."* All the hands were up. This group that only a few minutes ago believed that they could not swim 500 yards in an indoor swimming pool under ideal conditions, now believed that they could make that swim under very difficult conditions AND save a small child as well.

The lesson is - deep down, we all know that we are stronger than we show on the surface. We know we can draw on the power of our will if we have to. Why not *choose* to draw on that power because we *want* to?

Think about this. That child - out there at sea? That child is your gift. The unique gift that you were given at birth. It will die if you leave it out there, unattended and alone. This gift was entrusted to you. It is your responsibility. It's calling out to you. Go get it. Bring that child to shore, and live the life you were meant to live!

16.
Self-Discipline - The Next 30 Minutes

If you want to be successful, you will need self-discipline. Listen to any successful person, and they will tell you that self-discipline is the number one skill you must acquire to achieve anything great. This is so easy to understand and yet, so difficult to master - or so it would seem. But, is it really?

Look at the first paragraph of this chapter. Take notice of this sentence: *"Listen to any successful person, and they will tell you that self-discipline is the number one skill you must acquire to achieve anything great."*

Did you notice anything in particular in that sentence? Notice the word *"skill."* That word is very important. I believe that most people think of self-discipline as a personality trait, that it is something you are born with. I disagree. I know that self-discipline can be taught.

Self-discipline is *often* the byproduct of external discipline. Those who are raised with parental discipline typically have good self-discipline as adults. At this point I am sure that some of you are thinking of people who are examples which prove me wrong. It is true, not all children raised by strict parents grow up to exhibit quality self-discipline. Children grow up and choose their own path. (They're kind of like people in that way).

While it is true that there are many exceptions to the idea that parents can instill self-discipline in their children, training children from an early age to be accountable to themselves is a good place to start. As adults, we have to *want* to be self-disciplined, or this skill will not be well developed. The good news is, no matter when you decide to hone this skill, it can be done.

Watch, pretty much, any martial arts movie. Somewhere along the plotline, the protagonist will encounter some sort of conflict. Someone will do them wrong, and they want to get even. Enter the teacher (sensei). Our hero (the protagonist) is usually weak and undisciplined. The teacher trains the hero in the mystical, magical, martial art of choice.

The hero learns all about the origin and purpose of their art. They learn that with this new power, comes responsibility. The hero learns that true honor is achieved not through revenge but through forgiveness. (Final, honorable, butt-whooping scene for audience closure notwithstanding.)

The hero learns to master this beautiful artform through an action-filled and sometimes humorous montage. The student will become proficient in their new art within the duration of one pop song. (#1980's)

While this may seem a bit hokey, what is portrayed here is very helpful for our purpose. Through the use of the tool of *discipline*, the teacher was helping the hero to break the bad habits of their past. The hero was learning new, productive habits and creating a new mindset that would become useful in achieving goals in the future. The hero was learning confidence through self-discipline.

Once the hero saw the results of discipline, and the way they were able to transform their own lives using this tool, they are then able to add this tool to their toolbox. The tool of self-discipline is always available. Some of us simply need a sensei to show us it's value and teach us how to use it to our advantage.

In the martial arts movie scenario, we see how someone can be taught discipline, which can then transform into self-discipline. But, can we teach ourselves? (Good question) Absolutely!

How can you become self-disciplined? This is the easiest question for me to answer. It is easy because I had to teach myself. I know what it takes to learn this skill, I know what this skill can do for you, and I know how important it is to continually work on this skill.

I'll address these in reverse order. First, we must continually work on this skill. Self-discipline seems, at least for me, to be a perishable skill. I have used self-discipline to accomplish many things, but I noticed that I tend to be selective in my use of this great tool. If I am passionate about something, I seem to be able to focus on achieving my set goal by being disciplined. I make sure to keep working on the things I need to work on to get where I want to go. However, some things that I should be disciplined about, I am not. Over time, I become less disciplined in general.

My desk is a mess. I need to organize better and keep my work area neat. I have too many notebooks open, junk mail in my inbox, for some reason, and pens that are out of ink. Pens? Notebooks? (#Digitalnewbie) I need to clean this up. If I were disciplined with organization, I would have a neater work environment. I need to create a new habit of organizing my desk on a regular basis.

What all this means is, self-discipline is something that you need to work on regularly. Like martial arts, you must continually train, or your skills will fade. Have you ever heard the phrase *"exercise self-discipline?"* That's what you must do. Once you acquire this skill, exercise it to make it stronger. Like bodybuilders say about muscle, use it or lose it.

Next, what this skill can do for you has no limits. Just about every great thing ever accomplished was the result of self-discipline. Even things that the so-called *average person* looks to achieve, require self-discipline. Look at the following example.

Graduating from college requires the self-discipline to get to class, study and work when there is no one there to push you. In elementary school your parents made you get out of bed and get to the bus stop. They met with your teachers to find out how you were performing.

Your parents were there to make you do the things you didn't feel like doing. In college, it's all on you. Without your parents there to apply the discipline, you must have self-discipline. If you do, you will do just fine. You will do your work and graduate. The better you wish to do in school, the more self-discipline you will need to apply. It's that simple.

Lastly, a question: What does it take to learn this valuable skill? How can you develop this skill on your own? Well, since you will be as successful as you choose to be, we can assume you will be as disciplined as you choose to be. I mean, why not? Listen, I did it! *If I can do it, you can do it*, I promise.

The way to develop self-discipline is to choose a short-term goal. Decide what you want to do, then create a plan to reach this goal. This is what was discussed in the chapter on habits. You will use self-discipline to create the habit. You will force yourself to do what you have planned on doing. You will have to put in the effort to get going. Once you get moving, in the right direction, the habit will then take over and begin to pull you through.

Think of it like sledding. (WHAT???) Yep, sledding. Picture yourself on top of a snow-covered hill. The sled is just sitting still. If you were to simply sit on the sled, nothing would happen. You need a catalyst to get started. Now, lean over, grab the sled and start pushing. You will be walking, then jogging, then, once you get running and the sled has momentum, jump on and enjoy the ride! Gravity will take it from here.

That's how it works. You need the self-discipline (the catalyst) to get moving. Once you have created the habit, the habit will act like gravity pulling the sled down the hill. Give it a try. Use this plan for something simple. You will get a good feeling of what self-discipline feels like. You will also learn how habits make accomplishments much easier.

Here's one that I used to get the ball rolling. I bet you will come up with something just as easy. To keep my kitchen in order, I decided that I would no longer go to bed with dishes in the sink. It's a simple thing, I know, but I am much happier when the kitchen is clean. This is a simple task, but I had not always kept up with it. Now, I make sure the sink is clean before I go to bed. I start the morning preparing my coffee in a nice clean kitchen.

Once you have decided on the short-term goal, you need to create a plan. Decide what daily action you must take to reach this goal. Force yourself to do that thing each day. You must hold yourself accountable. Put it in your calendar and set notifications. No matter what you are doing, you must do the task you have set. This is the self-discipline needed to create the all-important habit. Try this for two weeks. See what happens. Experiment with more short-term goals.

You will get better at this as you go. You will begin to use the tool of self-discipline to achieve one short-term goal after another. Then, when you want to achieve a much larger goal, you will have the skills you need. As discussed with habits, simply break the long-term goal down into a series of short-term goals, and complete these goals, one after another. You'll be there in no time!

This chapter is called "Self-Discipline - The Next 30 Minutes" because the next 30 minutes is what makes all the difference. We have just established that long-term goals need to be broken down into short-term goals. The reason for this is so that we can prevent ourselves from becoming overwhelmed. Big goals can seem like too much when we look at them as a whole.

When a high school student thinks about earning a master's degree, this task may look like it will be too much for them. So, what the student needs to do, is create a plan, then focus on the first step. Get to class on time - every day. Take good notes - every day. Study - every day. If the student approaches school in this way, they will do fine. This tactic can be used for anything. Use self-discipline to create the habits which will pull you through each short-term goal. Now, let's see how you can get started.

The next 30 minutes are crucial. Every day, all day long, focus on just the next 30 minutes. That's where it all happens. That's where you will make your dreams come true. Can you see that? In case this doesn't make sense, I'll explain.

Procrastination is your enemy. The habit is your friend - and the hero which will deliver your dreams, as long as you use it to your advantage. Procrastination is the anti-habit. We tend to avoid the things we don't want to do, and the greater the task, the more we resist beginning. What if we changed our approach?

When I decided to write this book, I had nothing more than an idea. When this idea came to me, I put my two-part rule into action. Remember the rule? Part 1, if you have an idea, you have to take action on that idea. Part 2, once you start something, you must see it through, no exceptions.

Writing a book is quite an undertaking. When I first began writing, I decided that I would write 10 pages per day. Let me tell you, when you open up your computer and look at that blank screen and think, "Only about 50,000 words to go," it can be very intimidating. Getting started was by far the hardest part. But - I had my rule, and there was no turning back.

I needed the right mindset to get going. I used a trick that has always served me well. I use my "next 30 minutes trick." I feel like, no matter how difficult something is, I can handle it for 30 minutes. I can keep my focus and energy where I need it for that long. So, all I had to do was look at the clock and say, "OK, for the next 30 minutes I will write *something*. I was determined to begin a chapter and work on it for 30 minutes no matter what. It worked! Once I got started, I really got into it. I ended up writing for two hours.

I used this trick to begin whenever it was time to write. It is much like the way I forced myself to get into the gym each day before I had created that habit. This technique has proven very effective for me.

The idea is to create a mindset to get you moving. It is also a great way to help you avoid wasting time and doing things that detract from the pursuit of your goal. Let me share with you another way to use this trick. I say *"trick"* because I am kind of tricking my mind into propelling me forward. We have all let our minds trick us into putting our greatness off far too often and for far too long!

When you are going after an important goal, you should be continuously asking yourself: Is what I'm doing *right now* bringing me closer to, or taking me farther away from my goal? When you answer that question, you will know what to do. Once you know what to do, make a deal with yourself. *"If I do the thing I need to do, for the next 30 minutes, I can take a break."*

Once thirty minutes goes by, you will have either completed the task you set out to accomplish, built up enough momentum that you don't want to stop, (as I did while writing) or at worst, put 30 minutes of effort into acquiring your goal. In any case, you have made some progress and any progress gets you closer to your goal. You will also feel uplifted by your efforts, and you are building confidence.

Whenever you feel stuck, always ask yourself, *"What will I do in the next 30 minutes?"* Use this trick to get yourself moving forward. I also like to ask myself, *"How productive was the previous 30 minutes of my life?"* That question can be a real eye opener.

I know what the next 30 minutes holds for you. *Reading!* You're almost there!

17.
Don't be a Squirrel

Did the title of this chapter get your attention? I know it's strange, but watching squirrels provided me with a breakthrough in my thinking. I realized that I had been living my life like a squirrel. No, I did not climb up a tree and build a nest. But my behavior was very much like that of the squirrel, and I realized that these behaviors are very common, and unfortunate.

I grew up in an area with a lot of trees. I saw squirrels every day. I saw them, but I paid little attention to them. They did their own thing and never really bothered anyone. Nothing they did made any impact. I would see them climbing up and down the trees. They would transfer from one tree to another by jumping between the branches. I saw them rummaging in the grass for nuts to eat and materials to build their nests. Their existence was pretty mundane.

These squirrels were always there. They were always working. I would see them every day, all year long. Their behavior never seemed to change much. There were brief periods of excitement for these little creatures when our dog would chase them. (She never actually caught one, and I doubt she would know what to do if she did.) They would scramble up a tree and wait for our dog to lose interest. They would come back down and begin again, digging in the grass.

That was pretty much it for squirrel life. They did what was necessary to survive. That's all they ever did, survive. I thought about this. I realized something. That's what I had been doing - surviving. I was not ***living***.

I was living the life of the squirrel. (Ugh . . . sad.) All I ever did was what was necessary to get by. I worked, like the squirrel, to have food to eat and a place to sleep. I was not using my three gifts to actually, LIVE.

I went to work. I paid my bills. I ate and slept and went back to work. Round and round I went with no joy of life - like a squirrel. I had my dog-chase moments when things went wrong. My car would break down, and need repairs that I could not afford, or I would get laid off - again. Then, like the squirrels, I would scramble to save myself. Once the danger had passed, I would go back to digging in the grass. Was this it?

I remember thinking to myself, on many occasions - *"Is this all life has to offer? Is work, eat, sleep, repeat, all we are born to do? That's it? What the hell are we here for?"*

This never made sense to me. In my tiny world, this was all I ever saw. I never saw anything outside of this pattern, except for athletes and entertainers. Growing up, we had no internet. We didn't even have cable until I was in my late teens. We were not exposed to many interesting things.

I now understand why so many kids, myself included, wanted to be athletes, musicians or actors. These are the only people we saw that were not just working to survive. They were thriving. They were LIVING! Those were the only professions that many of us ever saw in which the professionals were doing something they truly loved. They had careers, not jobs.

What's the difference between a job and a career, you ask? A job is what you do for money. A career is something you would do if you didn't need the money. I *saw* that in football, but I have *found* it in speaking and writing. I love sharing my positive message of hope. I spent two years speaking for free because it gave me joy to give people hope.

I was not able to find that kind of joy working in the warehouse. While working as a copywriter was pretty cool, that wasn't quite it yet it for me either. As a manager, I was getting closer. When I was able to speak to an entire department, I was beginning to see my path.

But, when I talked to our stressed-out sales team, and they brightened up, I was hooked. I was able to give people a more positive outlook. They took my words and ran. People who were previously worried about failure, began to succeed at a tremendous pace. I can't take credit for their success, of course. This was their doing. However, their manager felt that my talk was the boost they really needed. She was very happy with the quick turnaround of her team. And as for me? I found my calling.

I found something that fed me. We all need to be fed. We all have a space within us that needs to be filled with achievement and productivity. We need to be useful, and we need something that drives us from within. I don't mean being driven to an end. I mean - we need to feel internally, compelled to *do*.

We search for these things and find them in a variety of places. Some people paint, some read, some cook and some volunteer. We find things that we are compelled to do. Many times, we find this in play.

Play is a learning tool. Lion cubs chase each other and wrestle. This play, is how they learn to hunt. For people, as children, play is how we learn physical and interpersonal skills. As adults, play gives us an outlet for our innate drive to compete. This drive keeps us sharp. It challenges us. We need to be challenged. Without challenge, we would fade away. There would be nothing left to live for.

That is one of the reasons so many people die shortly after retirement. Their drive was to do the job. They were challenged at work. Once that challenge was taken away, if they do not find a new challenge, their work here is done. They no longer feel needed. We need to be needed, wanted and challenged. If we are not needed, life has no meaning.

Look at how we seek challenge, simply for the sake of being challenged. Our hobbies can provide us with challenges. Some of us pay money to play golf, and we work hard to get better. Why? Is it important that we become better golfers? Of course not. It is merely important to have the challenge to drive us to improve. We need something to drive us.

When you find a job that drives you like that, you are already a success! A job that people do because it feels good, and they are compelled to do it, is a career. A good example of a career would be - teaching.

Teachers do not make a lot of money. Teaching is hard work. It takes commitment and incredible patience. This is also, an underappreciated profession. So, why would anyone do this work? Because, they are compelled. Teachers have to teach. It is the same way with musicians.

Let me demonstrate this idea like this. Musician, like teacher, is not a job description, it is a human description. It is not what they do, but who they are. If you drop a musician off, 100 miles into the wilderness, with nothing more than enough food for the journey home - during this journey, the musician will make music. They may sing. They may find some sticks to drum on their pack, supplies or trees, but they will make music. It's not what they do. It's who they are.

Teachers will teach. They will teach what they know to anyone who will listen. (Or read . . . hmm. This seems familiar somehow.) They are compelled to teach. It's simply who they are. If you take this away from them, you will destroy them. The same goes for the musician.

Years ago, I saw a heart-breaking story on TV. It was a piece on actor/musician, Dudley Moore. For those of you who do not know who Dudley Moore is, he was a short of stature, comedic actor. He was in a number of successful film comedies in the 1970's and '80's. He gained notoriety in the wildly successful 1979 hit, "10" starring Bo Derek. He was also a world-class pianist.

He starred in a movie called "Arthur" in 1981 wherein he played a millionaire playboy who drank too much. He took the role of the drunkard to new comedic artform. It became his "I'll be back" of Arnold Schwarzenegger fame. It was worked into many of his later films.

Years later, he became ill. He had been out of the spotlight for some time. In 1997, he had suffered a number of medical issues which affected his motor abilities. He was stumbling and slurring his speech. This gave some the impression that his characters were more real than an act. He suffered criticism and judgements. This was cruel and unfair. But what was most cruel and unfair, was not the way people of Hollywood talked about him, it was what the illness did to him. It took away his music.

I watched him in an interview discussing all of these things. When the discussion turned to music, the expression of agony and sadness on his face was brutal. He explained how, even though he was completely alert mentally, his hands no longer worked for him. He could no longer play the piano. He could no longer make the beautiful music that made his heart sing - that made him LIVE. As he explained this to the interviewer, he cried, so did I. I am crying as I type this.

Later in life, Dudley Moore's gift was taken away from him. This seems cruel. It is the reality of life. All things are temporary. We need to understand how short our lives are. We need to appreciate what we have and make the most of all we are given. This is what we were meant to do. It is what YOU were meant to do.

Seek out your gift. Develop it. Get everything you can out of it. Do not waste what you have been given. It's not too late, but someday it will be! Watching Dudley Moore cry over the loss of his ability to make music was painful. It made me feel like life is cruel. Now, I know better. He was given a gift. He developed it fully and used it to make his life beautiful. He shared it with others to enrich their lives and his own.

Was life cruel to take this from him? No. Life was completely generous to give it to him in the first place. What would have been cruel, would be if Dudley Moore had wasted his gift. He did not. The world is a better place for it.

I paid little attention to the squirrels. Nothing they did made any impact. You have amazing gifts. You have the ability to make an impact. What are you going to do about it?

Don't just exist. Live. (#NotaSquirrel)

18.
Fit for Success

Success takes hard work, commitment and focus. It also requires a great attitude, and the proper state of mind. All of these things take energy. In order to keep up with the demands of an achievement-oriented lifestyle you will need to be strong, both mentally and physically.

Reaching your goal will require working long hours. When we tire, we lose focus, and both work and creativity suffer. You know that you need to work on yourself. You need to be learning all the time. Your mind must be sharp. But what about your body? Is it really important for you to maintain a strong, fit body? Absolutely!

Why? What role does physical fitness play in professional success? There are two important ways that fitness, which contributes to your overall health, plays a part in your quest for success. These are; physical health, and mindset.

Let's begin with the most obvious, physical health. If you are physically healthy, and strong, you will be able to put in longer, more meaningful, hours working on your goal. I say *meaningful* hours, because it does you no good to stare blankly at financial reports while in a fatigued state. This is where mistakes happen. Let's try to limit those by being focused.

A rigorous fitness regimen gets your blood pumping and helps to increase blood flow. Keep at this consistently, and you will have better overall circulation, even at rest. This increased blood flow will move more oxygen to your brain which improves cognitive function. (Hey! We're thinking!)

You will also miss fewer work hours due to illness. If you are not taking care of yourself, when the doctor sees your blood pressure, he will tell you to back off of work. This happens all the time. Stay healthy, stay strong, and stay on track with your career.

One last important health note to consider. Why do you want all this success? Do you want to live a long, full life of enjoyment? Or, do you want to finance your 10 million-dollar, funeral? Think big-picture.

As for your mindset, a healthy lifestyle is a much happier lifestyle. Exercising releases endorphins into your system which gives you a natural high. I love the way I feel after a great workout. It always makes me feel so positive.

I learned the value and impact of a tough physical workout on the mind and performance, in college. I didn't read this in a book. I lived it. During my first semester in college, I was lost. By the end of the semester, I was afraid that I might actually flunk out. I needed to pull my grades up significantly with my final exams and papers. I had a great deal of studying to do and two huge papers to write. This Herculean task seemed beyond my abilities. I was a nervous wreck.

A friend stopped by my dorm room and asked if I wanted to go to the gym. *"Are you kidding??? I can't go to the gym now! I have too much to do!"*

"Come on," he said. *"A good workout will make you feel better. Besides, do you want to fail AND be small?"* (That was so wrong.)

I went to the gym. I was so stressed. I trained harder than I ever had in my life. For some reason, I just kept pushing. When my workout was finished, I was spent, (or so I thought). I went back to my dorm. I showered and dressed for dinner. After a quick meal, I returned to the dorm. Something amazing happened.

I looked at the pile of books on my desk that, a couple of hours earlier, intimidated me to the point of nearly cracking. Suddenly, I had a whole new outlook. I said, *"OK,"* I clapped my hands together. *"What's first!"*

I was not panicked at all. I was reinvigorated. I was so relaxed. I was able to study for hours. More importantly, I was able to focus. I tried to study earlier in the day, but I couldn't focus. My mind kept going to the fear of failing. All I was thinking was, *"I can't believe I am messing up so bad."*

That workout changed everything. I was able to study effectively. I went to the gym every day during finals week. I Killed it! All my grades came up. I was amazed at what I was able to accomplish. Now you see the psychological benefits you can get out of an individual workout. What can you get out of a fitness lifestyle?

One of the benefits I found, in taking the time to get proper exercise on a daily basis, was more time. I know that sounds counter-intuitive, but it's true. It seems that the more we have to do, the more time we have to do things.

When we are very busy, we are forced to budget our time. We have no choice but to improve our organizational skills. We plan better, and we become more efficient. We tend to create a rhythm and we build momentum. Have you experienced this in your life?

You get so busy that you have to start planning everything you will do, a week in advance. (I have a sneeze scheduled for 3:47 next Tuesday.) Once you get moving you can really get a great deal done. You have created momentum. You can schedule your workouts in such a way that they are a great compliment to your day. They can provide you with that pick-me-up or stress outlet when you need it most.

Another great benefit to exercise is confidence. I feel better about myself when I have a consistent workout routine. I feel like no matter what else is going on in my life, each day, I can do something positive. I am moving in the right direction in at least one area of my life. There have been times in my life where, working out was really the only thing I had going right for me. I needed it to keep myself together.

In addition to feeling good about doing something positive, I can tell you from experience, I feel more confident in my physical self when I am in shape. I don't know if it as much about how I look or more, how I feel. I like feeling like I can pop up out of the chair and get moving fast. I like feeling agile, rather than sluggish. I like the way my clothes fit when I am in shape. I just feel more capable and ready for anything. No matter what I am doing, I have an added sense of control.

If you do not currently have a workout routine, give it a try. I think you will like the results. Plus, getting into the fitness lifestyle gives you the opportunity to meet new people and expand your horizons. You may learn about all sorts of new and interesting activities that you may enjoy.

Some people go to the gym to walk or run on the treadmill. Some lift free weights while others prefer the machines. At most gyms there will be numerous aerobic and even aquatic classes to choose from. Some find that yoga changes their life in a meaningful way.

Those I know who have adapted the yoga life, (which is what it really becomes) are some of the most interesting people I know. They have really adopted a positive lifestyle.

While many people continually use social media to vent about things they don't like, my yogi friends (Is that how I say it?) always post positive messages and beautiful images of nature. They often post images of themselves in various yoga poses from all over the world. They all seem to be travelers. Very cool!

Since we only have one go-around in this life, let's make it worthwhile. You are striving to be your best, professionally. Strive to be your best - physically. You want to be around a long time to enjoy all of your success. Whatever you choose to do in this world, you should always strive to be your very best. Mediocrity in one area of your life can infect other areas. Worse yet, it can become a bad . . . habit!

19.
The Right Time to Quit

When you set out to achieve a goal, to fulfil a dream, and things aren't working out, when is it time to stop? When is the right time to realize - *"This isn't working out - I need to move on?"* When is it time to quit on your dream?

This is something everyone with a dream will have to answer. The road to success is not for the timid. You will have to do a number of things to reach your goal. Much of what you have to do will be difficult, challenging and often unpleasant. The reality is, most people simply are not willing to do what is necessary to succeed. So, they do not succeed.

In addition to all the work you do to reach your goal, you will also have to make many sacrifices. While friends are gathering and enjoying good times, you will have to say, *"I'm sorry. I can't make it this time. I have a lot of work to do."* You might as well make that your outgoing phone message.

You are not going to have time for movies, TV, happy hours, cookouts etc. One day, you will have time for these things, but that time will come when you are living the life you have worked so hard to achieve. Getting to that life however, requires that other things will have to wait.

You are committed to success, and so you get up early and you work hard. You make all the sacrifices and keep your nose to the grindstone. You keep at it. You keep at it. You keep at it. Time goes by fast. It isn't happening yet.

One day, your supporters will lose faith. Your money will run out, and your anxiety will begin to cause your chest to feel tight. Fear will grow within you, and the self-doubt that you believed you had overcome, will rear its ugly head. (Trust me, I know!) You'll think, *"My God, I'm failing! This can't be happening! What do I do?"*

This is the moment. This is what it's all about. This is what all of those motivational videos you have been watching for the last two years were talking about. What happens in this moment is what separates the 1% at the top, from the rest. You were all in, remember? You were all fired up. *"I can do this!"* You exclaimed. *"I can fight my way through anything. I want it that bad. I am willing to do whatever it takes to make it."* Remember? Well, now we shall see.

In life, everyone talks a good game. Everyone will tell you how strong they are. Everyone can take the hits. They are just that strong. Until they actually get hit. This is when you find out who you really are.

That is the reality of life. You WILL get hit. There is no way around that fact. Life is hard. It will test your commitment. In order to make it to the top, you must earn it. You need to prove that you are worthy of all the rewards you seek. Life *wants* to give you everything - but not for free. Life does not hand out participation trophies.

Life rewards effort, not wishes. All you want is waiting for you, but all the best stuff is on the top shelf. It is available only to those willing to pay for it. You pay with effort. You pay with sacrifice. You pay with sustained commitment.

Let me tell you what I know. When I have been rewarded in the past, my rewards came after the work was put in. I shared with you my love of football. It may seem trivial to some, but as a child, my aspirations were simple, and strong. I was committed to my goal, early on. I paid the price.

I took a lot of abuse. I was laughed at and ridiculed. I cried . . . often. The frustration seemed never-ending, year, after year, after year. I had to work hard. I spent so many hours in the basement, alone, working out. Once I decided that I would become a field goal kicker, I made a commitment to be my very best. I spent so many hours, for so many years, practicing - alone. I practiced year-round, in the rain, the cold, the snow. (The mailman quit before I did.) I wanted to be ready for anything, for any weather conditions. There would be no excuses. I would offer none.

As it turns out. I would need none. On a high school football field, on a bitter-cold and windy Friday night in 1982, my work paid off. Our football team was playing an away game. I jogged onto the field to kick a field goal. For some reason my coach called a time-out. I was standing on the field a few yards from the huddle. I was lined up to kick.

The players on the defense were all lined up looking at me. They were calling out to me. *"Hey kicker, miss it!"* I just looked at the goal posts. Wow. They were really far away. This was a 48-yard field goal attempt. The farthest I ever made in practice was 42 yards, and it was cold, and windy.

The announcers in the booth apparently took notice of the distance as well. They saw a 5-foot 3-inch tall, 129 lb. kid standing, ready to attempt the longest field goal in league history. I heard over the loud-speaker a voice with a chuckle in it. *"It appears, ha-ha that West,"* (My school was Central Bucks West) *"is going to attempt a field goal."* He laughed. (I'm tired of being laughed at.) In a few moments, no one would be laughing.

The whistle blew. The time-out was over. We set up to kick. I looked down at my holder. (I knew my center and holder would perform perfectly - as always. They were the best.) I gave him a nod. He looked to the center and put both hands up to receive the ball. *"Hut!"* . . .

On the last day of school, for seniors, I was outside of the high school. We were done for the day. I was walking down the sidewalk by the teacher's parking lot. It was a beautiful day. We had done it! We had finished our journey, and school was out - forever. This was both exciting and a little sad.

I ran into a guy that I hadn't really seen much since junior high. In high school we hung out in different crowds. We got to talking. We congratulated each other on graduating. We talked about what we were going to do next, college etc. Then he said,

"Hey, that was really cool when you kicked that record field goal."

"Thanks," I said.

He ribbed me a bit, when he jokingly replied, *"Ah, you got lucky."*

I knew he was just messing with me, but my answer came quickly and naturally.

"Maybe. But you know what? The more I practice, the luckier I get."

This is the way of success. I understand that this was just high school football. It's very small in the grand scheme of things, but it was significant in my life. It taught me so much. Football, as a whole, gave back to me more than I put in. Remember, we get back in life ten times what we put in.

I played a lot of positions on the football field, and I learned something different from each position I played. As an offensive lineman, I learned how to be a humble part of a team. The offensive line is a five-man unit that must work in harmony or else the team cannot succeed.

As a quarterback, I learned how to take on more responsibility and assume a leadership role. I learned that I needed to look out for my guys, and sometimes to take control of the huddle and keep the team calm when things were not going so well.

As a field goal kicker, I learned that success requires many, long, lonely hours of commitment. I spent so many hours lugging a bag of footballs to any goalposts I could find, to practice. I would kick hundreds of field goals at any given time. I created many drills and envisioned many scenarios. I worked extremely hard to perfect my craft. I rarely stopped before it was too dark to see.

I foolishly ignored injuries, and often found myself on my hands and knees screaming at the ground in frustration when my body betrayed me. All of these experiences taught me well. I learned the most valuable lesson when I was a kicker.

"What we do when no one is watching, is who we really are. It is that, which will make all the difference in our lives."

-**Wade Hoover**

As we learned from Wand Sykes, taking 20 years to become an overnight success, we can see that reaching your goals is a long and difficult process. Rather than doing great things now and then, we must, as stated earlier, do the little things every day that will eventually bring us to success.

My dream from childhood was to play football professionally. I made the move to kicking field goals because I thought that was my best chance to reach my goal. I worked hard, and I was able to play in high school, a little bit in college and also on a semi-pro team. But I did not make it to the professional level.

What then, is the point of my story? Why would I share a simple story of a kid playing football in high school? That's no big deal. I agree. But there is a valuable lesson here. You see, I was laughed at in junior high because I was so small that the idea of me on a football field was ridiculous. That, was without even telling anyone that I wanted to play in the first place.

Even though I was the last person anyone ever thought could play, I went further in football than anyone I grew up with. Here are my takeaways;

First, there is no need to listen to anyone else's opinion of what you can do.

Next, hard work and determination pay off.

And then, there is one more painful lesson that football taught me. You will regret quitting.

When I look back at how my football dream ended, I cringe. I feel regret. This is *my* big *"What-if?"* I'll never know the truth, and that is so hard to take. It makes closure very difficult. Was it really the dislocated knee that stopped me? How about the dislocated hip? (Now replaced) Was it merely the summer I spent trying a new technique that threw off my timing and caused my worst season ever? Did I really begin to lose my passion, or did I simply lose my confidence? What if I didn't walk away from my dream?

I'll never know If I would have made it, had I kept pushing. I achieved every goal I had set, up to that point. Whenever I was knocked down, I got up and worked harder. But in college, I had failures. I walked away from football. I still do not know the real reason why. I know that sounds strange, but I don't know if I truly lacked the ability, the drive, or the courage.

What I do know is, I regret walking away. I regret not seeing my dream through. I regret having to live with the fact that I quit. I regret that I never found out if I had the ability or not. I regret the *"What-ifs"* I have to live with for the rest of my life. I worked so hard and sacrificed so much for so long, and I'll never know what might have been. That is why I do what I do now.

I am writing this book as a plea. I am pleading with you. Please, PLEASE do not let this happen to you! I don't want anyone to feel like this. Believe me, you do not want to know what this is like.

Some of you already know the feeling of regret. It could be related to career, investment opportunities, relationships, just about anything. If you have that feeling, then you understand why I won't do that to myself again. I can't. It is too painful. Trying and failing may be painful, but quitting and never knowing what might have been is infinitely worse.

So, the answer to the question posed at the beginning of this chapter, *"When is it time to quit on your dream?"*

Answer: Never.

20.
Parole Yourself

By now I bet your head is spinning with ideas. You're thinking of all the things you are ready to accomplish. You should be getting to the point where you want to take on the world! But, will you? Are you ready to use the rule I shared in the chapter on Habits?

"If I come up with an idea, I must take action and begin working on my idea. Once I start something, I absolutely must finish what I started, no exceptions."

This will really help you move forward toward your goals much more quickly. What's amazing is, this rule is addictive and has quickly become, yes - a habit! I love it. This rule forces me to be so much more productive. Give this one a try. I believe that once you see how positively this affects your life, you will make this your rule too!

Alright, it's time to tie all of this together. If you want to make great changes in your life you will need to believe that you can. I mean, you really need to believe! Remember how we previously addressed *"Attitude?"* Your attitude is the most important element of success, and belief is what gives your attitude its power.

Your future success will emerge from within you. It won't come from an external source. You see, all of your obstacles come from within, so the necessary changes must come from within you as well. It took me a long time to realize this truth.

For most of my life I felt trapped. I really couldn't explain it at the time. I felt like I was in a prison cell. It was as though everyone else was in the world. They were living in the real world and doing things and living life. I, on the other hand, was stuck in this cell, looking out at them with envy. I felt so disconnected. I couldn't shake the feeling that I wasn't a part of society. I was a bystander - at best.

I hated the feeling that my only experience in life was struggling to get through one difficulty after another. I wanted to get past this feeling. I wanted to be a part of the world. I would watch movies and T.V. shows to escape my prison cell for a while. But then, the credits would roll, and I would once again turn my focus to the cold, unforgiving bars which separated me from the world.

My friends seemed to be doing well. They had problems too, but their troubles seemed temporary. Of course, everyone has problems, struggles and worries. But, if you only focus on these things, that will be your experience. (#LawofAttraction) That was me. My friends seemed to deal with their problems and then focus on what they wanted to do next. I preferred to focus on what bad thing may happen next. This was the problem. This is why I felt like I was in a prison cell.

Being in that cell was ruining my life. I wanted desperately to get out. I just couldn't figure out *how* to get out. Who was going to help me? I needed to file an appeal! I couldn't understand. How can I get out of here? Why am I not allowed to leave this cell? How did I even get here?

BAM! There it is! THAT was the right question. *"How did I get here?"* That is the question I should have asked many years ago. I couldn't solve the problem until I understood the problem.

Once I asked the right question, I was on track to finding the answer I needed. The answer to this question, as it turns out, is as simple as it is painful. Luckily, once I had the answer to *"How did I get here?"* I was able to solve the problem. I would soon be free!

How then, did I end up in this prison cell? Simple. I sentenced *myself* to life in that prison. That's right. I had done this to myself! I let my struggles make me gun-shy. I was like the little brother who flinches at the dinner table when his big brother reaches for the salt shaker. After so many years of being bullied by life, *and bullies*, I had retreated into my self-made prison cell. (#Comfortzone)

Afraid to try, afraid to take a chance, and afraid to live - I shuffled aimlessly through life, waiting to be knocked down again. I was the boxer who had been hit so many times that he simply covers up and never throws any punches. Yes, I had struggles, and we all do, but we can't let the past stop us from moving forward. I needed to see that prison cell for what it was - a pathetic construct of my own making.

The bars of this cell were made of nothing more than my own fears and self-doubt. The ceiling was merely my own self-imposed set of limitations. Like my panic attacks, I did this to myself, and so, I was going to undo it! It was time for me to take control of my own life. I did. I suggest you do the same. Like I always say, if I can do it, ANYONE can! That means *you*! You have everything it takes to live the life you want, the life you were meant to live. You have that power.

If you are not living the life you want, right now, remember one thing - You have the power to free yourself from the fear and self-doubt that prevents you from living that life. Your only limitations are the ones you accept. You have the authority to parole yourself. Do it. Do it today! Free yourself from that oppressive cell, and breathe the fresh air of freedom!

If this sounds too easy. If you are saying to yourself, *this guy is oversimplifying things*, then I would like you to consider another possibility. What if I am not oversimplifying things? What if **you** are **overcomplicating** things? Just consider that notion for a moment. What I am learning, more and more every day, is the greatest changes I make in my life are the least complex. The simplest alterations have had the most profound effects on my life.

To get better grades in college, I simply went to the library between classes to read each day. When I got into the best shape of my life, physically, all I did was exercise more and eat fewer calories. When I needed to land my first copywriting job, all I had to do was send out more resumes. When I wanted to help people, I simply volunteered. To overcome my stage fright, all I had to do was get on stage at open mic night. To write this book, I simply set aside a few hours each day to write.

When I put these very simple, and even humble, changes all together like this, it looks like nothing. However, these changes have enriched my life beyond measure. I am actually in awe as I write this. Until I wrote that last paragraph, I thought I was on to something. Now, I am blown away at the enormity of the power of these simple actions in my life. I was able to do this once I was able to accept responsibility for myself.

When you assess your life, look at where you are right now. Are you living the life you want to live? If the answer is no, then you are not living the life you were *meant* to live. You **can** live **that** life.

You may feel trapped and powerless right now, but I assure you, you are not. You may feel like you are life's spectator right now, but you are not. You are ready to break forth and make your dreams come true. The prison cell of your own creation can no longer hold you. Your dreams are real. This cell is not.

There is not one reason left for you to put off living the life you deserve to live. You are strong. You are ready, and it is time.

You are strong. You are strong enough to face your fears. You are strong enough to take on new challenges. You are strong enough to rise every time you fall. You are strong enough to set, and reach, your goals.

You are ready. You are ready to accept your dream. You are ready to move forward. You are ready to create your plan. You are ready to create new daily habits that will consistently move you toward success. You are ready to learn from failures and use them as tools to grow. You are ready to take all non-existent power away from your naysayers.

It is time. It's time to develop your unique gift. It's time to share that amazing gift with the world. It's time to grow. It's time to achieve. It's time to stop surviving and begin living! It's time to . . .

- Parole yourself. Free yourself from fear and self-doubt to live the life of success and abundance you deserve!

You can do anything you want because –

"You are stronger than you can possibly imagine!"
　　　　Wade Hoover – (The boy that everyone laughed at.)

www.ingramcontent.com/pod-product-compliance
Lightning Source LLC
Chambersburg PA
CBHW031923240526
45464CB00022B/672